IT'S ABOUT
PEOPLE

Other books by Jim Hohnberger
with Tim & Julie Canuteson

Escape to God

Empowered Living

IT'S ABOUT PEOPLE

HOW TO TREAT OTHERS,
ESPECIALLY THOSE WE DISAGREE WITH,
THE WAY JESUS TREATS US

JIM HOHNBERGER
WITH TIM & JULIE CANUTESON

Pacific Press® Publishing Association
Nampa, Idaho
Oshawa, Ontario, Canada
www.pacificpress.com

Designed by Linda Griffith
Cover art copyright © by Darrell Tank

Additional copies of this book are available by calling toll free
1-800-765-6955 or visiting http://www.adventistbookcenter.com

Scripture references are taken from the King James Version
unless otherwise marked.

Library of Congress Cataloging-in-Publication data:

Hohnberger Jim, 1948-
It's about people: How to treat others, especially those we disagree with,
the way Jesus treats us/Jim Hohnberger with Tim and Julie Canuteson.
p.cm.
Includes bibliographical references.
ISBN: 0-8163-1964-2
1. Church controversies. 2. Evangelistic work. 3. Christian life.
I. Canuteson, Tim, 1963- II. Canuteson, Julie, 1967- III. Title.

BV652.9 .H64 2003
248.4'.86732—dc21
2002192585

04 05 06 07 • 5 4 3 2

DEDICATION

To all those who, like me, have experienced

the heartache of personal rejection because you see

things from a different perspective; because you dare

to conduct your life outside the normal sphere of

others' expectations; because you value freedom

more than friendships when the price would be a

trampled conscience; and because you value

people over and above policy or politics,

this book is dedicated to you.

CONTENTS

PREFACE

The book you hold in your hands is not a book of theology, theories, intellectual ideas, or even the product of extensive research, but rather a book of my own, often bitter, experiences. For I believe it is important for you, dear reader, to understand that I write not as one who has arrived at the experience for which he longs, but as one who has fallen into many of the devil's sand traps, and if, by sharing my experience, I can spare you a trap or two along the way, then I have achieved my goal.

I grew up in a nominally Christian household, by which I mean that we attended church and believed in Jesus, prayer, and the doctrines of our church. Although my family's understanding of God shaped the strong morals of right and wrong that my parents diligently instilled in those of us privileged to grow up in their home, religion remained only a part of our life, something neatly tucked away for Sundays and occasional holy days. I was a sensitive child with true spiritual longings, but much to my disappointment, I never knew in any personal way a God who loved me.

Only as an adult would I find out that the Bible taught the truths of God very systematically, and I fell in love with God's Word. I still didn't know God, but I was raised, as I said, with clear ideas about right and wrong, and when I saw that the Bible taught one thing and my family believed differently, I set out earnestly and zealously to straighten them out! I knew what the Bible taught, and I was determined to fix up my family's theology. So I took God's Word and used it to beat them up. I Bible-thumped them but good, and they didn't like it. They wouldn't accept my truths, and I was baffled.

Years later, as the Lord has moved me into a full-time ministry for Him, I find my doctrines haven't changed, but my attitude toward those who don't hold them has changed. I have also found that there is no shortage of people who are determined to straighten out the preacher. Others have felt, and continue to feel, the need to let me know my mistakes. After a single sermon I may be informed that I have been too hard, too soft, too theological, not theological enough, told too many stories, repeated a story, or worse, smiled in the pulpit! I looked wrong, acted wrong, dressed wrong, prayed wrong, or in the opinion of some, have been just plain wrong! Now I welcome any input, for surely I know I am a weak and failing human being, but most detractors are not content to share concerns and leave me to the care of God. No, they want to help Him out a little and force me to change into their ideas and notions of what I should be or do, and then if I don't cooperate with them, they reject me.

In short, I have been the persecuting and the persecuted, the offender and the offended. So I find myself uniquely qualified to present to you *It's About People*. If there was anyone who ever needed the message of this book, it was I. Yet I am not unique. Every one of us, to one degree or another, has made the same mistakes. The churches are filled today with junior holy spirits determined to fix up those about them. The number-one reason people leave the church is that another member offended them. Should we be surprised? It is well past time that we started asking ourselves some very hard questions about the way in which we relate to one another. If we can't get along down here with those we claim as brothers and sisters, we will not get along up there. If something doesn't change in the churches and in our lives, this whole discussion will become superfluous, for we will never see the kingdom or have another chance to get along with anyone.

CHAPTER 1

IT'S ABOUT PEOPLE

"But he turned, and rebuked them, and said, Ye know not what manner of spirit ye are of. For the Son of man is not come to destroy men's lives, but to save them" (Luke 9:55, 56).

I awaken near midnight, sensing a presence in the room. Wide-awake now, I listen to the sounds of our wilderness home, as it, too, seems to be resting from the day's activities. A gibbous moon looms majestically over Glacier National Park, headed westward to set beyond the Whitefish Mountains. The quiet is so loud you can almost touch it, with only the distant yip of a coyote disturbing the peaceful setting we love so much.

The moonlight through the windows illuminates our room and gives the familiar surroundings an ethereal look, but the mists of dreamland hold no appeal for me. I have a visitor awaiting my company. I sit up, trying not to disturb my sleeping wife, and turn my attention to my audience with the King of kings.

I had been meditating recently on Calvary. It wasn't the first time. For years, I had longed to understand it more fully, to experience it more deeply, and I had been praying for many months that God would reveal its mysteries more fully to me. Now I sensed God's presence in the room. It was nothing I could see or hear, but I sensed that God was there, and He had chosen that particular time to give me a larger glimpse of Calvary. The panorama spread before my mind's eye, and I was there. I could see it all; and what God showed me that night, I now share with you.

It is a beautiful spring morning in Jerusalem, and the sun greets the city with a blast of brilliant light that promises heat. The streets are jammed even at this early hour, due to the Passover. Thousands of pilgrims throng the nation's capital. The attention of the people seems riveted on some event now taking place, and a cohort of soldiers on escort duty catches my eye. They are leading three prisoners to execution, slowly forcing their way through the hostile crowds.

Hostile crowds are nothing new to Jerusalem's garrison. The Jews are a proud, independent people, and the sight of Rome's banners on the walls rankles the populace, which makes no secret of its hatred of Roman rule.

Yet, today's crowd seems to bear little enmity toward the legionaries. No, today it is the prisoners who garner the public's spite. Only the most despicable of criminals are disposed of in this manner, and even the Jews, who despise being under Rome's heel, approve the government's method for the demise of *these* criminals. The mob sends both insults and saliva in the direction of the condemned men.

I watch as Jesus is led down the crowded avenue. He is lean from travel and ministry, but still His form reveals the strength of a craftsman. He is visibly weakened by His all-night trial and repeated beatings, but His bloodied form awakens no sympathy from the onlookers, who jeer and mock Him with words and pelt Him with stones.

I walk behind Jesus, following as close as I dare. Suddenly He glances back at me, and for a moment our eyes meet. I can contain myself no longer. "Look at them," I cry, gesturing toward the crowd. "They laugh at You! They don't even care!" I am appalled, disgusted, and revolted. I want nothing to do with those sinners who could greet a man's dying with such a carnival atmosphere. To them it is just a big joke—no, it's worse than that. They think they are preserving their nation from this revolutionary. I am ready to write them off.

But then Jesus turns to me and with seriousness I cannot mistake, rebukes me, saying, *"It's about people, Jim! The gospel is about taking poor, lost, mixed-up people and restoring them into My image. Jim, it is not just about holding up truth and pointing out error, as you have tended to think. It's about restoring those very people who are spitting on Me right now."*

There in the quiet of my room, as the scenes of Calvary fade from my view, Jesus asked me four questions in the recesses of my mind. Their echoes have lasted through the years, their impact on my life, my ministry, and my relationship with others continually growing, as I realize the love Christ had for me, for all of us, and how far below His standard is our puny love for others.

"Jim, what would you have done with Aaron? You remember Moses' brother, the one who allowed the golden calf to be built by the children of Israel while Moses was up on the mountain speaking with Me and getting the tablets of stone with the Ten Commandments? We could refer to him as the vice president of God's denominated church. What would you have done with him?"

I could picture the whole story in my mind. Aaron had been left in charge while Moses was on the mount. Problems started when Moses spent far longer on the mountain than the people expected, and they came to Aaron saying, "Make us gods, which shall go before us; for as for this Moses, the man that brought us up out of the land of Egypt, we wot not what is become of him" (Exodus 32:1). So, Aaron asked them to bring him gold jewelry, and then he melted it down and made a golden calf for the people and told them that this was the god that had led them out of bondage.

Then later, when confronted by Moses, he denied responsibility and claimed all he had done was toss the gold into the fire and by a miracle, out came that calf. Think about it. Aaron was left in charge, but he led the people into sin. He explicitly disobeyed God and made a false god—an idol. Then he had the nerve to lie about the whole affair. What would you do with a national or church leader who had been involved in such a scandal? I know what I would do. I would throw him or her out, and I bet you would too! We'd make sure that person never had a position of responsibility to misuse again. What did God do? He made Aaron the high priest. The gospel is about restoring those who are weak in character, not throwing them out!

Then God asked me, *"What would you have done with David? King David, who not only committed adultery, but to cover it up, murdered a man. What would you have done with a leader like that?"* We would throw him out, but God didn't. Yes, there was need of reproof and repentance. However, not only was David restored to the throne, but also through his union with Bathsheba, another man's wife, God brought forth the royal line of Solomon and eventually Christ Himself.

The third question God asked me that night was, *"What would you have done with Peter, self-confident Peter, who cut off the ear of the high priest's servant with a concealed sword?"* What did Jesus do with that ear? He restored it! Whom do we resemble? Are we like Peter, chopping off ears? Or like Christ, bending down and picking up the ear and restoring what was harmed? Not only did Peter cut off the servant's ear that night, he denied his Lord *three* times! What would you have done with Peter? I would have said, "There's nothing we can do with that guy. There's no hope for someone like that. Throw him out!"

What did Jesus do with Peter? He turned and looked at him, and it broke Peter's heart. Can you just imagine the love in His eyes, the drawing out of His heart in sympathy toward the one who was denying Him? That single look spoke volumes. It said, "Peter, Peter, you're trusting in yourself. Put it all down and surrender it to Me. I want you, Peter. Give Me your heart." That's the gospel of Jesus Christ. His gospel seeks for the restoration of the erring—all the erring.

The Lord continued on, *"Jim, what would you have done with Saul before he became Paul?"*

I was starting to catch on to what the Lord wanted me to see, but this was too much. "Lord," I said, "Saul was the worst persecutor of God's people in his day. He made life miserable for them! Surely I'm not supposed to try and restore such a one as this . . . am I?" What would we do with Saul? I don't like to think about it, but Christ took Saul and made him into Paul, the greatest evangelist the world has ever seen.

The gospel is about taking these kinds of people, transforming them, and then using them to reach the world with the same gospel that has reached down and changed their lives. We as a people seem to have missed it, but the gospel is a whole lot more than a system of truths, the opposition of error, or even which church you attend. It's about the redemption of those who don't see it our way or who are antagonistic to our truths, our church, or our lifestyle.

Do we have the real gospel, friend? What are you doing with those who don't see things the same way you do? What about those with whom you differ in your own church, those in other ministries, or institutions? What are you doing with those who don't agree with you? What is your attitude toward them? You know, there is a tendency in our hearts and in our lives just to discard them, to put them on the trash heap, toss them away, to write them off, to count them out. But is that the gospel?

Are you involved in activities of tearing down and throwing out? Those attitudes and activities have nothing whatsoever to do with the gospel. In Romans 10:1 Paul says, "Brethren, my heart's desire and prayer to God for Israel is, that they might be saved." Paul wrote this after he had been beaten, stoned, whipped, and thrown in prison by his brethren, and yet he showed an attitude of love toward his enemies. His only desire was that they might be saved! Paul understood the gospel. There was within his heart a longing to reach those who persecuted him. He did not regard their case as hopeless in spite of their conduct.

Listen to the words of another author on this subject. "There can be no more conclusive evidence that we possess the spirit of Satan than the disposition to hurt and to destroy those who do not appreciate our work, or who act contrary to our ideas" (*The Desire of Ages,* 487). If our attitude is to destroy those who don't agree with us, whether they are in the church or some other ministry, we possess the spirit of the devil. Strong words? They aren't mine; they are God's own testimony. I see this attitude manifested today. I see it in the church of God. Members and leaders alike promote it. It is prevalent outside the organized structure in ministries. It permeates institutions. And it scares me to death! It scares me because it has nothing to do with the saving gospel of Jesus Christ.

I know that there are those outside the organized church who have attacked the church, and the church has responded and attacked them in kind, until trying to unravel who started it all is an exercise in futility. More important, everyone is missing the point—and incidentally, the gospel as well. "Far better would it be for us to suffer under false accusation than to inflict upon ourselves the torture of retaliation upon our enemies" (*Thoughts From the Mount of Blessing,* 17).

So how does God expect us to deal with such situations? Galatians 6:1 states: "Brethren, if a man [the term *man* here is generic; we could easily substitute *church* or *ministry* or *self-supporting institution*] be overtaken in a fault, ye which are spiritual, restore such an one in the spirit of meekness." If someone is overtaken in a fault, they may not understand the truth the same way we do. Perhaps they have a misunderstanding about something or are unbalanced in their understanding, but whatever the cause, you who are spiritual should restore such a one in the spirit of meekness.

Spirituality is not judged on the basis of certain fundamental beliefs. *Spiritual* does not mean those who have the truth and can teach it to others. *Spiritual* does not mean that I can tell you about prophecy. Even the devil can do that! The text says, "ye that are spiritual," not "ye that are knowledgeable." Too many of us think that because we have knowledge, we should go out and correct others. But when we do this, we are totally missing the boat.

Being spiritual means that one is under the control of the Spirit of God, that one's life is led under the guidance of God through a living and vibrant, moment-by-moment relationship with Him. "In the spirit of meekness" means that self has been put to death and we work for others, not caring whether we get hurt, because our only concern is for the lost soul.

There is a lot of enthusiasm in the church of God to work for Him, but all too often it is the sort Paul spoke of in Romans 10:2: "For I bear them record that they have a zeal of God, but not according to knowledge." Paul was certainly qualified to recognize false zeal. He had been out there persecuting those who didn't see things the way he did. Paul was personally acquainted with misguided, unbalanced zeal. I see a lot of it out there today, with well-meaning people trying to correct other people, churches, and institutions—all in the name of truth.

A typical statement I hear is, "Our testimony has to be even more pointed than was that of John the Baptist." I agree with the statement, but there is a problem. The problem is that we cannot give the John the Baptist message unless we have the John the Baptist experience.

I spoke with a man one day who was the leader of an independent ministry, and he told me, "God has raised me up to give the John the Baptist message!"

His wife was standing there, and I turned to him and said, "May I ask your wife a question?" He agreed, but looked at me sort of funny, as though he were wondering what Jim Hohnberger was up to. "Ma'am, I want to ask you an honest question. Does your husband live the John the Baptist experience at home?"

"No."

"Then, sir, God has not called you to give the John the Baptist message." How could I say that? Because we are told that John the Baptist had risen to the height of self-abnegation. Self did not appear in John's life, but in this ministry leader's life, self was ruling all the time. The gospel is not just about pointing out error or even preaching truth, but in restoring people to their Savior. You cannot restore others when you yourself have not been restored. We must find a balance.

Yes, there is a time to hold up truth, and, yes, there are times we need to point out error, but there is also a time to love and save the people. These three must blend together, as they did in the ministry of our Lord and Savior, Jesus Christ. Jesus taught the truth. He taught it so well that people said, "Never a man spake like this man" (John 7:46). He pointed out the error, even chased the merchants from the temple, but He loved the people. He would pass through towns, healing every one of the people's diseases, and He loved His enemies so much that as they drove the spikes through His hands, He was praying, "Father, forgive them for they know not what they do." What an attitude of love our Lord displayed!

How very different from the attitudes displayed in the next story. It was almost time for Jesus to die, and He was on His way to Jerusalem. To get there He had to pass through the village of the Samaritans. He sent James and John ahead to make reservations, if you will, at the Samaritan Inn. So they went on ahead and asked for lodging for their Master, but their request was refused. The Samaritans replied rather haughtily, "We'll have nothing to do with him, because he is on his way to Jerusalem—to the organized church."

James and John were furious with the reception they received and demanded of Jesus, "Lord, shall we bring fire down from heaven and destroy them?"

Jesus looked at them sadly and rebuked them. "Ye know not what manner of spirit ye are of. For the Son of man is not come to destroy men's lives, but to save them" (Luke 9:54-56).

The Samaritans represent what I would refer to as the "independents" today. They believed in the coming Messiah and they believed in the Word of God, but they were separate from the organized body. When they found out that Jesus was not coming to spend time with them but was on His way to spend time with the organized church of their day, their attitude was: "We won't have anything to do with Him." Have you ever seen that attitude in the church today? I have. There are some ministries that won't let me speak at their meetings because I speak in organized churches. That's the only reason. What kind of attitude is this? Is it from God or the devil? Do you know there are some churches that will not let me speak to their congregations because I speak to independent ministries? Again, the only issue that concerns them is where I have preached, not what I present. Our attitudes reveal an awful lot about our Christian experience. Are we missing something important? I believe we are.

We are told that, "Of a truth I perceive that God is no respecter of persons" (Acts 10:34). Does God love the independents as much as He loves the organized body? Of course He does! He reaches out to us regardless of the color of our skin, our nationality, our denomination, or our affiliation with certain ministries. He is willing to mix with all of us. Have we missed that attitude? Oh, we have fearfully missed it. "Had [Jesus] come to restore the temple and worship upon mount Gerizim, they [the Samaritans] would gladly have received Him" (*The Desire of Ages*, 487). In other words, it was as if they had said, "Hey, if you'll just be one with us, if you'll think the way we do, if you will just join our group and have nothing to do with *them*, then we are glad to receive you." What a selfish attitude! It has no place in the gospel today whatsoever!

I was asked to speak once at a large independent camp meeting with some rather controversial speakers. I prayed about going because I knew if I spoke there, I was going to be misunderstood. "Lord, do You really want me to go? If You do, I am willing to go and preach the gospel to those brethren." I felt impressed to go, and while I was there, a leader of one of those controversial ministries was there. I had never met him in person, so I approached him and said, "Brother, I have never met you. Do you have a few minutes where we could go for a walk and get to know each other?"

He looked at his watch and said, "No."

"Not even five minutes?" I persisted. "I'd just like a chance to get to know you a little bit."

"Well, maybe five minutes," he finally conceded, and together we started down the road. We hadn't traveled a hundred yards when he turned to me and said, "Jim Hohnberger, I don't trust you!"

"Why? You've never even met me before."

"I hear you've been speaking in organized churches."

"That's right," I responded.

"I also see that you've been speaking at some of these other ministries that we don't agree with," and he named them.

"Yes, that is true," I commented.

"Well, brother, you've got a foot in both camps, and I don't trust you!"

I silently prayed, *Lord, give me wisdom and give me the strength to speak as You would have me speak.* "Do you want me to tell you why I speak in both 'camps,' as you put it, and why the Lord has given me permission to do so?"

He looked doubtful, but nodded. "Because they both have the same problem you do. It is called 'self,' and it is rising in you right now." This opened up a really interesting conversation dealing with the real problems of the Christian life. You see, he thought "they" were the enemy to be resisted. A lot of sincere people think this way. They think the organized church is the enemy, or those ministries that don't agree with them are the enemy. Who's the real enemy? *Self.* Your self and my self are the enemy, and if we haven't found the victory over self, we have no business going out and attacking those other "enemies."

The *saving* gospel is about people, restoring people such as Aaron, David, Peter, and Saul. No knowledge of truth, however correct, demonstrates that one possesses the gospel. This man, I am sad to say, did not possess the gospel of the Lord Jesus Christ, despite the fact that he was a ministry leader and a man others looked to for spiritual guidance. He had what I call "intellectualism." That is what we have when we make a truth, any truth, into *The Truth*. And from that perception comes the attitude that anyone who holds to our truth must certainly be one of the enlightened people, and those who don't must be the enemy. This veneration of certain truths apart from a concern for people is error. Nowhere in Scripture is this taught. Yet, all of us have met people who are riding their particular hobbyhorse, and if you don't see it the right way, which of course is their way, then they write you off as a hopeless case.

How does God relate to such an attitude? We are told, "The very essence of the gospel is restoration" (*The Desire of Ages,* 824). What does that mean? Would you restore a car or a house that is in perfect condition? It wouldn't make any sense, would it? No, it stands to reason that whatever is in need of restoration is going to have a few problems, maybe even a lot of problems. So, those whom we are asked of God to try and restore are not likely to see things the same way we do. They may not view truth the way we do. They probably won't conduct their family in the manner we would and their lifestyle will differ from us as well. But could we even possibly hope to restore them if we reject them because they have warts and problems and don't see things the way we do?

This exclusivity is found not just outside the church, among the independents, but inside the church as well. There was a church leader in another state who had managed to block a number of my speaking engagements, and one day I felt impressed to give him a call—to try and develop a dialogue, some sort of understanding between us. I reached him by phone, and he immediately took over the conversation.

"Jim, I'm just going to tell you right straight out. Unless you agree to absolutely have nothing to do with them," and he named "them," which happened to be a number of independent ministries, "you will not speak in this conference!"

If I would not accept his policies, then I was to have no place in the ministry. Policies are what we bureaucratically call "partisan decisions," which the less sophisticated among us call by their right name, politics, and they have no place in the gospel and should find no place in God's church. You see, this minister's entire focus was on his policy. In this man's frame of reference, whatever the system says, you must do, and if you don't, you're out! This is the same attitude that caused Christ to be crucified. The religious leaders in His day thought surely it was better that one man die than to sacrifice the whole nation.

"Sir, I'd like to give you a reference in Scripture for the position I hold," I told the man. "It's Revelation 14:6. We are to take 'the everlasting gospel . . . to every nation, and kindred, and tongue, and people.' I see no exceptions to this at all! If we possess the gospel, really possess the saving gospel, we won't refuse to take it to those who don't have it. It makes no sense that if our church possesses the gospel that saves people, we would then as a church policy decision withhold it from those who, by your very admission, need it the most."

Friend, this man didn't have the gospel either. He had in its place partisan politics; it is a condition I like to refer to as "churchianity." "Churchianity" means we line up with a system rather than lining up with Jesus Christ.

Let's go back to the story of the Samaritans rejecting Jesus when He wished to lodge with them. Remember that James and John wanted to destroy them with fire from heaven. They were two of Jesus' closest followers and had been with Him for years. Surely they knew about the gospel. They had watched as Jesus restored men's lives again and again, yet they wanted to destroy those who didn't see things their way. I find this same attitude in the church today, and it shakes me to the bone. When we hold that attitude and then as a body of people pray for the outpouring of the Holy Spirit, God help us! Save us from ourselves! Please, Lord, don't give us Your Spirit, not when we have this attitude.

What did the disciples want to do? What would they have done if empowered with the Holy Spirit? They would have destroyed the very people whom Jesus came to save. You see, God can't give us His Spirit while we hold this attitude, and we had better stop praying for it and start praying that self will be hid with Christ in God and that the rule of self in our lives may be broken. The attitude we harbor toward those who disagree with us demonstrates whose spirit we possess. James and John were "Christians," yet they had quite a way to go in learning to put self to death in their experience. In this story, they were demonstrating the spirit of Satan. If you and I have been involved in some way in activities that manifest this type of spirit, if we have cassette tapes, or videotapes, newsletters, or magazines manifesting this spirit, we must get rid of them, friend. It doesn't matter where they come from. Wrong is wrong, no matter if it comes from within the church or from outside it. Because by beholding we become changed. Get it out of your homes, run from it as fast as you can, because it will corrupt you, and it is absolutely opposed to the gospel of Christ.

Jesus was pained by the words of James and John. He was on His way to die for those very people His disciples wanted to destroy. The gospel is about people. It is not merely about doctrines or a system; it is about the people for whom Christ has died. The gospel is about restoring lost souls for the heavenly kingdom.

I believe that we as a people have a problem. We seem to love "the organization" or "the truth" more than we love "the people." This spirit to hurt and destroy a person, a system, or a ministry, is not of God. If we are ever to qualify to enter the kingdom of God or to be used of God to reach others, we had better let God bring some balance into our approach.

When I was introduced to the Scriptures, I had never read them before, and I was amazed! I said, "This is truth! This is light! This is something I can conduct my life by." And it was! I fell in love with God's Word, and I wanted to share it with others. So I started sharing. One of the first people I went to was my devout Roman Catholic mother. I was eager and zealous, and I told her, "Mother, did you know that you don't have to pray to the saints? And Mother, did you know infant baptism is not taught in Scripture? And Mother, did you know that we are reading from the wrong Bible? And Mother . . . and Mother . . . and Mother . . ."

Did my mother say, "Praise the Lord. My son has found the truth"? Not in the least! I met with resistance—a brick wall, and cold reserve. I thought, *I must have approached it wrong.* So I went back a couple of weeks later with even more zeal and the wall went up higher. My family rejected me and would have nothing to do with my newfound love.

Four years later, the Lord asked me to sell our home and business and move 1,600 miles to the wilderness. God made it clear to me that while I had left off some of the worldly things in my life and had gained knowledge of the truth, I was still holding that truth in unrighteousness. I had left the world, gained hold of truth, and found the church, but God had to take me up to the mountains to show me that self was still ruling in my life. After two years in the wilderness God told me, *"I want you to go back to your parents' home, and I want you to stay with them for a week."*

"I can't do that, Lord! Even when I was living near them, we were estranged."

"Jim, when you walk in the back door of that home I want you to go up to your mother, and I want you to put your arms around her. I want you to hug her, kiss her, and tell her you love her."

"Lord, I can't do that! You don't understand. We're German. We're stoic. We're austere. We love, but we never show the affection."

"And then, Jim, I want you to go over to your father. I want you to put you arms around him and hug him and kiss him and tell him you love him."

"I won't do it, Lord! It's too hard!"

A month later I found myself driving 1,600 miles toward my parents' home. When we arrived, I pushed my sons and my wife in the door ahead of me. I was going to try and delay this for as long as possible, but at last there was Mother before me. I went up to Mom and hugged her and said, "Mom, I love you." She clung to me as she embraced me and wouldn't let go! The tears rolled down her cheeks; it just broke her heart. You see, in my whole life I can't remember ever doing that with my mom before. I had never hugged her and never told her I loved her. Instantly, Mom knew I was a new creature and that there was something different about this visit.

After I finished hugging my mother, I saw my father standing there, watching all of this. I went over to him, and he froze stiff as a board, not sure what to do. I wrapped my arms around that stoic old German and gathered him in. I told him I loved him and kissed him, and when I let go, I could see the glint of tears in his eyes as well.

God had told me, *"Jim, in your visit I don't want you to ever once mention Me, or My Word. I want you to clean their attic, paint their living room, trim the hedge, and take them to the store. I want you to minister to their needs.* "So that is what we did. We did everything we could to help them out. After five days, one of my brothers called me and said, "Jim, can we go out to eat this noon?"

I said, "Sure," and we agreed on a place to meet.

We had barely sat down when he blurted out, "What are you doing to Mom?"

"What do you mean?" I was genuinely baffled.

He said, "I've never seen Mother so happy in all her life. What are you doing?"

"I'm just living the gospel I believe, instead of preaching it."

"If that's what it takes," he continued, "then do it and don't stop!"

Not that long ago, I was invited to my hometown to present some meetings in my old church. I stayed with my parents that week, and they have come to know the messages God has laid upon my heart. When the week was over, they took me to the airport so I could catch a plane back to Montana. My mother got out of the car at the curb in front of the terminal. She's elderly now and walks with a cane, so I was kind of looking down at her. She fixed her gaze on me and said, "Son, I want to tell you something. I agree with everything that you are doing. You have found Jesus!"

What made the difference, friend? The difference was that I loved the people as much as my special truths and God's church. They sensed I loved them—unconditionally—and when they saw and felt that, then they wanted my gospel. It is only as others see that we really love them unconditionally and that we are ready to serve them, that the gospel will have true saving power in our life. Why? Because the gospel is about people!

CHAPTER 2

ISSUES, ISSUES, THE ISSUE

"Keep thy heart with all diligence; for out of it are the issues of life"
(Proverbs 4:23).

Before I came to know God in any real and practical way, I used to let my mind roam from subject to subject at random. I didn't care whether I was thinking about new reports of government corruption or whether I contemplated the upcoming season for the Green Bay Packers, but all that changed when I heard about the Bible, joined a church, and, in the understanding I had back then, thought I had become a Christian. Suddenly I had new thoughts, new desires, and new wishes. Christ was wooing me, courting me, if you will. He was desirous of winning my affections, and let me tell you, I was ready for them to be won. I had longed all my life to know God, and now I felt at last that God was accessible to me.

In my study I learned just a little bit about a man named Enoch. The Bible says Enoch "walked with God," and a real burning desire was born in my heart to do the same. What must it be like to live your life here in the flesh with such a living, vibrant connection to God that is so strong, it is as though you were walking together minute by minute, day by day? *Wow!* I thought, and Enoch became my hero. I longed to experience just such a relationship with God as he had.

The enemy of our souls knew that at this point if Jim Hohnberger was to gain the secrets of Enoch's walk with God, he was in danger of losing his power over me. He knew I was starting to fall in love with the things of God, and if something wasn't done immediately, I might move from an intellectual love of the things of God and fall in love with God Himself. Hence, he was very quick to introduce me to what I call "issues," the biggest sand trap around. Satan could no longer use the appeal of all the old worldly pleasures and distractions against me because my new love for the things of God's kingdom had displaced them. Therefore, he employed the subtlest of distractions. He used my own love and interest in the things of God to derail my budding Christian experience.

I had been attending church for all of three or four months when we were visiting at someone's home after church. There were a dozen or so members present, and animated conversations about spiritual matters flew back and forth freely. Remember, I wanted to learn more about Enoch, but as I listened, a man brought up a topic that really caught my ear—John Todd and the Illuminati and secret societies and organizations. "What is this about that Illumina—whatever you call it?" I piped up. I had never heard of such a thing, and it piqued my interest and aroused my curiosity.

I had wanted to study about Enoch, but I got involved in studying about the devil's secret societies, and it didn't stop there. Pretty soon, I began to wonder whether there were members of these great conspiracies around every corner and all throughout church organization. It took me about a year to explore that topic thoroughly, and I emerged to realize it hadn't helped me in the least.

Finally, I was ready to start studying Enoch when a new controversy came up, this time in my own denomination. A theological controversy had been ignited relating to our understanding of faith and works. Now, I didn't even know in any practical sense what faith was. I still didn't know how to surrender my will to God or even how to exercise faith, but I had accepted a position of leadership in the local congregation. Therefore, I felt the need to have an understanding of the issues involved, so I undertook a study of both sides. Without being grounded in the most basic and babylike article of Christianity, I was in no way fit for leadership or qualified to participate in theological discussions, yet there I was taking a position on all the issues swirling through my church, and it took away another year while my spiritual condition languished.

Then one day I received a newsletter from some person on the fringes of Christianity, alleging a cover-up of the facts regarding a certain historical event in the church, which took me off for another six months. Meanwhile, Enoch was still waiting for me. Then there were problems regarding a certain church book and whether it portrayed our doctrines properly. That took me off for another few months while Enoch waited and my relationship with God, my spouse, and my family declined.

I don't know whether you have ever seen a dog race, but I am told they have this mechanically operated rabbit that the poor dogs must chase around the track. And they chase it, every time half knowing it is fake, knowing they can't catch it, knowing that there is nothing in this chase for them, yet they still run after the thing. And that is exactly what I was doing!

I don't know what spiritual jackrabbit the devil has you chasing right now, but I have chased enough of them to guarantee that every six months or so, there will be another one. The devil has to keep us too busy for Enoch, too busy to latch on to God, too busy to realize that we're running in circles. And all the while he and his imps are entertained by our foolishness.

Satan wants to get us chasing after every sin in the church, every doctrinal error, every crazy new concept, every new man who prints a newsletter and claims to be called to a ministry, all because he is a lot smarter than most of us, and he knows that there is no saving good in any of those things. The saving good are things that draw my family and me closer to the heavenly kingdom. But if these things don't change you, don't transform your marriage and reform the way you relate to your children, then they amount to no saving good.

There are always going to be lots of good things and good people who waste our time, distract our focus, and discourage true personal piety, while making a pretense of religion. Now I am not saying you are doing these things. You may be, but I am telling you that I have done these things. Let me share with you the way it was for me.

The church I attended chose me to be head elder, and I took my responsibilities seriously. I felt the need to understand all the issues floating though the church so I could instruct the people, but this had unexpected consequences. I was home one day sitting in my recliner with a whole stack of materials on these issues when my oldest son came up to me and said, "Father, can we go out and play ball?" A boyish grin danced across his face.

"Matthew, don't bother me right now! I've got important things to study. Don't you know I am the head elder of the church, and I've got to know these things? Please play by yourself for a while." His shoulders slumped and the light of anticipation drained from his face right before my eyes as he turned and walked away. "He's just going to have to understand," I muttered, excusing myself.

Another day and in similar circumstances, my son Andrew came to me to see if I would go out and play truckie with him in the sandbox. He loved it when I would get down in the sand with him and all his trucks and bulldozers. Let me tell you, we did some serious earth moving out there. You could even hear our engines roar *vrooom!* as we made roads, airports, and mountains of sand. But this day I was trying to study the issues, so I put him off. "I can't right now. I've got to learn all this stuff, so I can lead the people at church. Don't you understand? The people depend on me."

So, my sons languished, my marriage languished, and Enoch still waited for me. And more important, the God of Enoch waited to talk with me, to love me, and to change me, but everything else seemed so much more pressing and vital for my spiritual development. I played the fool, and I am not the only one, for Romans 1:18 describes such ones as I as "[holding] the truth in unrighteousness." There are many in the church in the state that I was. We have the truth, but what good does it do us? We argue over it, scrap over it, churches divide and split over it. Even families divide and separate over it. Are we really walking with God when we do such things, or do we just think we are walking with God?

God finally decided to wake me up to the idea that perhaps I wasn't all I claimed to be, and He sent me into the mountains, into the wilderness, to find Him. I had to sell my house, my cars, my business, and give up all my worldly security to try and find Him. Friend, there is a cost to finding Jesus; let no one tell you otherwise. If you really want to walk with God, it is going to cost you dearly of the things you love. Christ Himself told stories of the men who had to give all that they had to possess the hidden treasure and the pearl of great price. We can't buy our salvation with the things we give up, but we'll never find the One who bought our salvation while clinging to them.

When we moved to the mountains, the Lord had to deal very firmly with me because I was a very hard case. I thought that I would arrive and be like Enoch in six months. Little did I know that it would take me more than six months just to come to understand that the problem wasn't my wife! It took me years, I mean *years* to deal with this stubborn flesh. It takes years for most of us to grab hold of learning to walk with God. Moses, Paul, John the Baptist, and a whole host of other biblical heroes, all had to spend time in the wilderness learning how to handle the flesh we are born with. If you think you are the exception to the rule and that you're going to somehow magically grab hold of God when the crisis comes, good luck! We are not exceptions to the laws of heredity. Every one of us is fighting, to one degree or another, the same ailments of character, which are part and parcel of being a sinful human being.

We all tend to seek spiritual fulfillment from what we believe, instead of what we are becoming through the grace of God. Our beliefs may be absolutely correct, yet if the world looks at the man who holds them and doesn't see those same truths in his life—well, you get the idea.

My friend Tom and I had just arrived to speak for several days at a large gathering of Christians held on the grounds of a lovely camp. We were walking toward our cabin when a voice intruded into the peaceful setting.

"Jim Hohnberger! Jim Hohnberger! Is that you? Hold up! Wait for me. I must see your face!" my white-haired pursuer called.

We turned to see an older man in his late sixties. He was dressed simply, although he appeared somewhat disheveled after his eager pursuit of me. His craggy face bore a determined look. I glanced at Tom as if to say, "This is going to be interesting."

"Finally!" he gasped, as though he had been looking forward to this moment for quite some time. "I've got five questions to ask you!"

"Well," I said, setting my suitcase down on the pathway, "go ahead."

"Number one is: What is the one text from the entire Bible that is the foundation of our faith?"

I looked at Tom, who said, " 'I can do all things through Christ.' "

"No!" he snapped out, as though irritated because Tom quoted this vibrantly confident pronouncement of faith. He then fixed his gaze upon me and commanded, "You tell me, Jim Hohnberger."

"Acts 17:28: 'For in him we live, and move, and have our being.' "

"You're wrong!" He barked and proceeded to quote a proof text for a denominational doctrine.

"What's your second question?" I asked.

"Did Christ take upon Himself the fallen or the unfallen human nature?"

"What's your third question?"

"Was the atonement completed at the Cross?"

"And your fourth?"

"Are babies born sinners?"

"What is your fifth question?"

"Will we continue sinning until Christ returns?"

I had been praying throughout this encounter that God would give me His grace and His wisdom because I don't have all the answers. Now I turned to him. "I have just one question for you before I answer your other questions. Brother, do you believe that I can be a conservative Christian, active in outreach and witnessing activities, take the gospel to the whole world, answer all five of your questions correctly, and still have no living experience with Jesus Christ, not be changed into His likeness, and not go to heaven?"

His countenance just fell. At first he was confused and visibly frustrated, then the frustration turned to anger, and he stomped off without another word. Well, this wasn't the end of the story. After preaching there for three days, a group of three acquaintances called me over to talk with them.

"Jim, what's this we have been hearing? Someone told us you don't believe it's possible to have victory over sin?"

Now, I've preached a number of messages over the years and have been accused of a lot of things, but never of that! "Gentlemen, can I guess where this came from?" Then I described my white-haired interrogator of the first day.

"How did you know?" they asked.

This man was missing something in his experience, and while our list of issues might be a little different from his, he's still a vivid warning of an incomplete Christian, of faith without practicality. We have to be sure the same thing isn't missing in our lives. I have to be honest with you; there are many even among those who preach the truth to others who are not going to be saved! They are not preaching error, nor are members of the "wrong" church. They understand every point of truth and even know the will of God. And yet they don't have corresponding works.

The thief on the cross couldn't have answered my white-haired friend's questions, but the thief's heart was surrendered to God, and that's all God wants. He can fix our theological problems if, and only if, we give Him all our heart.

Let's look at how Jesus dealt with the issues in His day. If there was ever someone besought with issues, it was our Savior. He faced theological and personal issues continually, not to mention the societal issues and injustices that screamed out for change. Yet, He never entered into the conflict. Do you think that perhaps He understood some things you and I have been slow to perceive?

Jesus was well into His ministry by the time the events occurred that are recorded in Luke 20. He had rocketed into the national spotlight many months before by healing all manner of diseases, preaching, casting out demons, and seeking in a quiet, yet determined, way to correct the philosophy, pet theories, and teachings of the religious leaders and point the people back to God. This quiet opposition excited the animosity of the Jewish leaders, who were unused to having their authority questioned, let alone disregarded by someone from the lower, uneducated classes. So here they all are at the beginning of Luke. I can picture it all in my mind as they gather themselves together in their costly doctoral robes with their staff members and scribes, planning to easily overcome Jesus by means of subtle questioning. To make sure everyone hears of His defeat, they invite the elders of the people to come along.

Luke reports it this way: "The chief priests and the scribes came upon him with the elders, And spake unto him, saying, Tell us, by what authority doest thou these things? or who is he that gave thee this authority?" (Luke 20:1, 2). Now here is a question every religious leader can relate to, for no religious body is totally free from self-appointed preachers. The very question raises troublesome questions for us today.

Jesus had no earthly authority. God appointed Him for His work, and He possessed none of the usual qualifications that men look for, such as degrees or lengthy internships. No organization backed Him, and no great men sponsored His ministry. His ministry was to the poorest classes—the prostitutes, the drug users, and thieves. Men well known for their bad tempers were His associates. He kept company with those who could ruin your reputation. He mingled with both the rich and the poor, in the best neighborhoods and the worst. He feared no diseases, and He was a friend to those who were viewed by the religious leaders as suffering under the curse of God for their sins. Perhaps a modern-day parallel might be homosexuals who have Acquired Immune Deficiency Syndrome. Bring it home to yourself today. How would you or your church organization respond to a self-appointed minister who hung out with skid row bums, women of questionable character, and whose associates and followers sprang from the lowest classes of society? Furthermore, what would you think if this man became the best-known minister of your denomination and appeared in the newspapers and magazine features that speculated openly about whether he was the long-hoped-for leader to save the nation? In truth, almost everyone in the Jewish church from leader to lowliest member had already drawn a conclusion about where Jesus' authority came from, and these leaders knew it. They had the express purpose of pulling Jesus into controversy and hopefully removing from Him the mantle as God's messenger that the common people had gladly placed there.

But Jesus "answered and said unto them, I will also ask you one thing; and answer me: The baptism of John, was it from heaven, or of men?" (verse 3).

Christ didn't jump into their trap, play their game, or try and convince them of His position. He instead brought them back to the itinerant minister they had rejected earlier, allowing the Holy Spirit to thus bring conviction upon their hearts. He wanted them to see their errors and repent before they rejected Him in whom was life itself, but they dared not be so honest, even in their refusal to believe. "They reasoned with themselves, saying, If we shall say, From heaven; he will say, Why then believed ye him not? But and if we say, Of men; all the people will stone us: for they be persuaded that John was a prophet. And they answered, that they could not tell whence it was" (verses 5-7).

Jesus looked at them. Their clever answer was utterly transparent to Him, and He replied, "Neither tell I you by what authority I do these things" (verse 8). But Jesus wasn't yet done with these men. There was still a heart-wrenching love in His heart, an overwhelming desire to save them from themselves before it was too late. So He turned back to the people around Him and launched into a story as if He had resumed preaching, but His aim was to reach these men who had come to Him in hate.

Jesus told about a certain man with a vineyard who "let it forth to husbandmen" (verse 9) and went into a far country for a long time. As time went by and he was due to receive the produce, that is, the income, from the vineyard, he sent his servant. But the husbandmen beat him up and sent him away empty-handed, and they did the same to a second and a third servant.

> Then said the lord of the vineyard, What shall I do? I will send my beloved son: it may be they will reverence him when they see him. But when the husbandmen saw him, they reasoned among themselves, saying, This is the heir: come, let us kill him, that the inheritance may be ours. So they cast him out of the vineyard, and killed him (verses 13-15).

Thus Jesus vividly portrayed to these men their course of action. They had rejected messenger after messenger sent to them from God, and now they were on the verge of rejecting God's beloved Son whom

He had sent to them. By the time Jesus finished His discourse, "the chief priests and the scribes the same hour sought to lay hands on him . . . for they perceived that he had spoken this parable against them" (verse 19). But they could not do so at the time because "they feared the people."

Now isn't the authority behind Jesus' mission important? Yes, it is, but not as important as His mission itself, which was to reach the heart of men, including those who were His adversaries. Because reaching hearts was His only desire, He refused to enter into controversy and debate. What about us? Are we eager to prove our positions and defend our beliefs? Are we truly Christlike? I wonder.

How did the religious leaders of Christ's day respond? "They watched him, and sent forth spies, which should feign themselves just men, that they might take hold of his words, that so they might deliver him unto the power and authority of the governor" (verse 20).

They wanted to trap Him. They decided to twist His words and comments and thus bring about His death, just not at their hands, they hoped. It would be much better to have what politicians refer to as plausible deniability. Then they could claim they had nothing to do with it. They could point out that it was, in fact, the Roman government that killed Him. Their course would be blameless. They had even tried to warn Him that His teachings would get Him in trouble, but He had rejected their good counsel.

The next thing they decided to use to trap Him was a good ol' standby—money! Even churches today are often filled with contention over the issue of money. Where should donations go, and what should be done with them? In every denomination, there are those who would dictate to others their duty before God, and in certain circles those who would dictate your duty toward the civil government as well. Certainly there was no shortage of opinions relating to the subject in Christ's day, yet these learned men came to Christ as if seeking after knowledge. "Is it lawful for us to give tribute unto Caesar, or no?" (verse 22) they queried.

"But he perceived their craftiness, and said unto them, Why tempt ye me? Shew me a penny. Whose image and superscription hath it? They answered and said, Caesar's. And he said unto them, Render therefore unto Caesar the things which be Caesar's, and unto God the things which be God's" (verses 23-25).

Money is an important issue; please don't misunderstand what I am about to say. Money is a talent. All of us will be required to give an account to God for our management of the means He has entrusted to our care, but as important as this issue is, Christ understood something very few of us in the church seem to understand—namely that it is an issue between the soul and God. Christ knew that there were men among those leaders who went to the extreme in paying tithe on every iota of income, yet not even ten percent of their hearts was given to God. He also recognized in some of the Gentiles about Him, honest souls who had never given of their substance to God, yet had hearts that were fully given to God's control. Therefore, His reply was designed to address the root issue in the hearts of His questioners. Am I rendering unto God all that is His? This question goes much deeper than the surface issue of taxes. "And they could not take hold of his words before the people" (verse 26).

Sometimes I think, and in fact I am sure, that you and I are too quick to share our words, to speak up when questioned, to defend our position and our beliefs. We sometimes feel that is our duty to defend God as if He were not capable of taking care of Himself. Like Peter, we pull out our sword to do battle, and like Uzzah, we put forth our hand to protect the ark. But the hard truth is that God doesn't need us to defend Him, and if Christ Himself was very circumspect about what He, as God's Son, said, it would follow that in His example lies a significant message for us, would it not?

"Then one of them, which was a lawyer, asked him a question, tempting him, and saying, Master, which is the great commandment in the law?" (Matthew 22:35, 36). This man, an expert with words, had carefully planned his exchange. If Jesus named any one of the ten as the greatest, thus discounting the others, there were people nearby who would condemn Him for blasphemy and stone Him on the spot. It was a clever trap, and the results of a poorly thought-out answer could be fatal.

"Jesus said unto him, Thou shalt love the Lord thy God with all thy heart, and with all thy soul, and with all thy mind. This is the first and great commandment. And the second is like unto it, Thou shalt love thy neighbour as thyself. On these two commandments hang all the law and the prophets" (verses 37-40).

Isn't His answer beautiful in its simplicity? While grand in its comprehensiveness, the answer contained nothing the lawyer could grasp hold of to entrap Jesus, and once more the efforts of the leaders were stymied.

Next they turned to a favorite ploy of intellectuals since the first man who decided to call himself a scholar, and test Jesus' ideas by human reasoning rather than the Word of God. They invented an "unexplainable" hypothetical situation. As is usually the case, the scenario was designed to reinforce the arguments of the scholar whose position has weak biblical support. The Sadducees came to Jesus with a rather improbable story, which just happened to reinforce their belief that there is no resurrection. Their tale went like this:

"Master, Moses said, If a man die, having no children, his brother shall marry his wife, and raise up seed unto his brother. Now there were with us seven brethren: and the first, when he had married a wife, deceased, and having no issue, left his wife unto his brother: Likewise the second also, and the third, unto the seventh. And last of all the woman died also. Therefore in the resurrection whose wife shall she be of the seven? for they all had her" (Matthew 22:24-28).

Talk about ridiculous questions, but perhaps it's not any sillier than many questions on which we waste time today in the churches. "Jesus answered and said unto them, Ye do err, not knowing the scriptures, nor the power of God" (verse 29). Do you think Jesus might say the same thing to us today? "Ye do err." Put away the issues you are contending for; they have little value.

I was invited to speak one weekend in Ohio. The mother and children of the host family gave us a warm welcome, but as the husband wasn't home from work yet, we visited a little, and then moved to the living room to await his arrival. The home returned to its normal flow of activity. We watched the children in their play, and my heart ached a little as I watched their squabbles, realizing that no one had taught them how to overcome their upset feelings by surrendering them to God and letting Him remove them. About this time the husband drove in, and we heard him enter the kitchen where the wife was finishing up a few tasks. I don't know what she did to displease him, but he just lit into her, and we could hear them going at it in the kitchen. I couldn't help feeling uncomfortable, so I got up and strolled over to the window for something to do, all the while praying the Lord would soften their hearts. The children were arguing right beside us in the living room, just like their parents were doing in the kitchen.

Right next to me was a rack of tapes, and it caught my attention. I read the various titles, and it was like a "who's who" of issues in the church. Alongside of it was a video rack filled with videos containing all the trash, trivia, and trouble that take place in the church today. There was also a little basket there on the desk full of papers, and as I glanced around I realized it was full of scandal sheets and garbage-collecting newsletters. You know the type I'm talking about, the ones where the sins of the church are explored in depth and the leaders are castigated publicly so that the readers feel better about their failings. These dear people had been filling their minds with garbage, religious garbage to be sure, but trash is still trash. If they had taken all the time and energy they spent studying the misdeeds of the church and put it into finding Jesus, they wouldn't have been fighting out in the kitchen nor would their children have been following their example. Do you see yourself in this picture? If you have allowed junk like that in your home, the devil comes along with it. I do not need to know all the errors in the church, as long as I know the truth and am connected to Him who is the Truth.

I've got a friend who is so involved in all this stuff that he is hiding up in the mountains. He sends out a newsletter talking about the problems in the church and the rumors of the government—of concentration camps, of plans for executions, fears of secret attack, and of government agents in black helicopters. If I read his newsletter, I wouldn't be able to prove or disprove any of it by the Word of God because it is all speculative and all in the future. How can you argue about what hasn't happened yet?

It is our job to present the truth. The truth is not rumor, not wild-eyed extremism, which grasps any twist of fate as part of an underhanded plot; nor is the truth so-called intellectualism, work that seems designed to instill doubts rather than to create faith in the things of God. The truth as it is in Christ is balanced. It is simple and basic, yet challenging on a very personal level to the most intelligent person. The truth is not a fuzzy intellectual reality that we can debate after church or in a college lecture hall, but a life-changing, practically applied knowledge that we are in a battle to the death with no one more dangerous than ourselves. And if we haven't been learning to win this battle, there is absolutely no value in any of our eloquent opinions, for they cannot save a single soul.

This friend of mine who publishes the newsletter has studied every issue in the church and the government, so that it seems as if he has a Ph.D. in this trash. If I want to know the latest rumor about anything, I can just call him, and he will have heard about it. However, my well-informed friend has a problem—he has not won the hearts of his wife and children, nor has he convinced their minds and souls that he is a Christian—far from it. That, my friend, is the truth, and it applies not just to my friend but to the entire church.

I have never found one man involved in this kind of junk who has a good marriage. Not one! And they all seem to lose their children! So what good does it do them? What do we really have to say to the world if our gospel, our truth, is such that we cannot even see it instilled in our own children and have their lives restored? I know this is not a popular position, and there may be a rare exception to the rule, but our children are the fruit of the home, and by their fruits you shall know them.

The temptation is always before us to deal with the issues of our day, because these are the trivia of life, and as long as we deal on that level, we don't have to deal with the issue of our own hearts. Over and over we see Jesus refusing to play the surface-issue game. The Samaritan woman at the well tried to draw Him off by bringing up the issues between the Jews and her people, but He brought her back to issues of her own heart by asking her to bring her husband.

The man let down through the roof was different. He wanted forgiveness even more than healing. Jesus read the desire of his heart and forgave his sins before He healed his ailments. Repeatedly Jesus took the very ones rejected by His society and offered them a new heart and a new start, while the religious ones, like you and me, were left out in the cold. He could do nothing for them because of their satisfaction with theoretical knowledge. Most of us have knowledge of truth, yet we do not possess a heart experience.

Satan has filled the world with things to capture our attention and our time. If you are one of the few in the church who have severed your ties with the world, don't worry because Satan has filled the church with controversy and corruption sufficient to occupy your attention forever! Christ did not try to straighten out His church because He knew it was a losing battle. But do we try? You can't fix the problems in the church. You can't do it! What about your own home? What about your own life? Is every problem in these areas corrected through the grace of God? Have you faithfully dealt with everything the Lord has shown you that needs to be surrendered to Him? If we have not, then why do we deceive ourselves into the notion that we are supposed to correct the church and reform our brothers and sisters? I'll tell you why; it is because in so doing we are able to put off the work of sanctification necessary in our own hearts. Jesus knew that even He could not change a corrupt priesthood, and we think *we're* going to—good luck!

Jesus took the gospel to the souls who were hungry for it. He had time to reach harlots and, yes, even government employees, considered by many as part of some conspiracy. Jesus didn't think that way. He longed for the hearts of tax collectors and Roman soldiers. He was focused upon others, instead of Himself. Because of that, He reached out to the very ones others feared. If we have the gospel, my friend, we will not be found fearing some type of nebulous plot because we know nothing can happen to us without God's permission.

Heart work must be made the great work of life, and everything else must be subordinate to this. The enemies of Jesus demonstrate the utter folly of trying to do the work with only an intellectual understanding of truth to guide them. If that's all we have, it would be better for us to do no work along religious lines until we correct this deficiency.

Once a man came up to me and said, "Jim Hohnberger, you're crazy! Are you saying we ought to stop all our outreach until we get this right?"

I said, "Yeah!"

"All our mission fields?"

"Yes."

"All our books and magazines?"

"Yes, friend; you've got the idea."

He looked stunned, so I continued. "If we get our priorities right and make sure we really have something to share before we share it, we could finish the work in just a few short years. But if we continue as we are, it is an impossible task that will never get accomplished. And our Lord and Savior Jesus Christ will have to make the same pronouncement to us that He made to the church leaders of His day: "Ye compass sea and land to make one proselyte, and when he is made, ye make him twofold more the child of hell than yourselves" (Matthew 23:15).

Nicodemus was, the Bible tells us, a ruler of the Jews who came to see Jesus by night. Nicodemus had an agenda. Undoubtedly, he wanted to find out for himself whether Jesus was the Christ, the Messiah. There was no question that this man was the most influential person to come to Jesus at this point in His ministry, but Christ did not enter into Nicodemus's agenda. Instead He went to the heart of the issue with Nicodemus and dealt with the true need in His hearer's life.

If you or I had been there instead of Nicodemus, what would have been our agenda, and what would Christ have said to us? What has He been saying to you through His Spirit as you have been reading this chapter? Would you dare to go to Jesus with your issues? Are you going to blame your problems all on your husband or wife? Let me tell you that Jesus will lay the soul bare, and there will be nothing you can say to excuse your dabbling in these useless issues.

Christ doesn't care about issues, but, oh, how He cares about you, your spouse, and your family. His heart breaks for the families of the church as they have educated themselves in issues but don't have so much as a preschool certificate in surrender and dependence upon Him. He only wants us to be happy and to enjoy our relationships with others. He wants us to be able to relate to others the way He does. Wouldn't that be better than what we do currently? Typically we use the old "feel-them-out" process to find out where they stand on our issues before we'll accept them. The choice is ours to continue in our puny and petty issues or to enjoy the extravagant love of Christ and the friendship of all men.

I have given up my issues. This does not mean I do not believe certain things, for certainly I do, but through the grace of God I have placed these things below the level of my concern for the salvation of others, and I pray that through my poorly expressed words and imperfectly enunciated theology, the Holy Spirit will encourage you to make the same choices I have. The gospel is not about issues, but about people just like you and me, who are dying for want of a kind word and an understanding heart to listen, really listen to their heart's cry for love. And amid our church today, awash with issues and conditional acceptance, who will answer that cry? May you answer, "Hear I am. Send me!"

CHAPTER 3

THE SPIRIT OF THE LORD, OR THE MARK OF CAIN

"Where the Spirit of the Lord is, there is liberty"
(2 Corinthians 3:17).

Attitudes are a truer guide to the condition of our heart than many of the outward displays of Christianity, so often mistaken for the genuine article. What is our attitude toward others? The title of this chapter identifies two attitudes, contrasted in the Bible as opposites. There is the Spirit of the Lord, and there is the mark of Cain, and we are operating under one or the other of these.

What was God saying when He inspired the Bible writer to pen these words, "Where the Spirit of the Lord is, there is liberty"? If we have the Spirit of the Lord, there will be the spirit, of liberty surrounding us. If we are truly partaking of His Spirit, there is freedom and elbowroom. We give one another the latitude and the space to be individuals. There is no coercion and no force in God's attitude. God does not exercise undue control and does not believe in intimidation or in manipulation of others. Liberty is the freedom God allows everyone in the formulation of thoughts and the resultant lifestyle changes those thoughts may create.

If God grants *us* such liberty, those who are under the control of His Spirit must exercise the same consideration of others that our Lord and Savior exercises toward each one of us.

Recently, I became acquainted with a family that has been studying the health reforms, and they are making some changes. They had always been vegetarians, but now they were eating and combining their foods a little differently from the way they had in the past. Their fellow church members had noticed these changes, and some of them had made it clear that they didn't approve and were more than a little uncomfortable with the changes they were pursuing. Friends, the question is not whether the diet changes were right or wrong. The question is, are we willing to give them the freedom to explore and pursue what they see as their duty, while at the same time loving and accepting them, even if we do not agree?

You see, when someone is exploring and pursuing new areas, they may become unbalanced, and the natural tendency of other human beings is to get in there and straighten them out. But most of us don't quite have the nerve to do things that openly, at least not if our first hints in that direction are not well received. So, what do we do? You know, don't you? We go to others, and we talk about the family in question, and we start pulling away from them. This is just what was happening with the family I visited. Their fellow church members began pulling away, and the talk started going around. "Watch out! Better stay away from them. They are turning into food fanatics. Did you know about so-and-so? Yeah, those are the ones. Nice family. It's hard to believe they got these principles wrong." You know how it goes.

Do you know what the Lord brought to my mind as they told me their story? He reminded me of all the times I have done this very thing to other people. So, don't get the idea that I am saying self-righteously that you do this and I don't. I am saying that the Lord has reproved me in this area. If His Spirit is speaking to you, my friend, we are in the same boat. I am the kind of person who sees things very strongly in terms of right and wrong, black and white. And, of course, I have that natural human tendency to think I am always right! Therefore, when I see you doing some-thing that I feel is wrong, I'm naturally reluctant to grant you the liberty to follow your convictions. Instead, I'd like to impose mine on you.

Liberty is a serious issue because if we don't come to understand liberty the way God understands it, we are going to continue to accrue just as rotten a record of violated rights in the remnant church as in some other denominations we tend to view with disdain because of the way they have trampled the liberty of others. Liberty requires that we allow each person the freedom to follow the dictates of his or her conscience without our applying some form of external verbal or behind-the-scenes control.

"Those Hohnbergers, they're not coming to church quite as often as they used to. I hear they are staying home some weeks. I wonder whether they are becoming separatists." And so the rumors spread about Sally and me almost twenty years ago. The truth was, if anyone had bothered to inquire, Sally and I were not withdrawing from anyone or anything. We had simply come to the point in our Christian walk where we started asking ourselves, "Do we really have what we think we have?" We weren't staying home because of antagonistic feelings or theological conflict. We were earnestly seeking after a Christian experience that we didn't fully understand and were just beginning to realize was missing in our lives—in spite of our reputations and positions in the church. Running my own business gave me such a busy schedule that about the only time we had for quiet reflection was Sabbath, and the endless round of church activities did not lend itself to such introspection. So we took some Sabbaths off, just by ourselves, where we could talk and be open to the impression of God's Holy Spirit.

I know of no text in the Scriptures that commands one to spend every Sabbath in church, yet that is how most of us have come to view Sabbath keeping. Therefore, when Jim and Sally don't come every week, even though they are keeping the Sabbath by the biblical standard of seeking after God and spending the day with Him, the tendency is to look disparagingly at them because they don't do things the way the majority do. Even with something so basic to Christianity as church attendance, we need to give one another the liberty to pursue God as individuals.

We tend to think that if others don't view things our way, or if they don't come to our meetings, they must be fanatics, separatists, and backsliders. The problem with such thoughts is that much of what masquerades as Christianity is only form. Perhaps some of our friends who didn't understand what we were doing would have been better off staying home to seek God rather than leading out in the services. The real point is not how we view the issue of attendance, but whether we are going to allow one another the liberty to do things differently and to follow a different pathway, while still loving and accepting one another. God is the Author of religious liberty, and if we are ever to reflect His character, then we are going to have to start learning to emulate His characteristics. He never compels, never coerces. He says, "If you love Me, keep My commandments." God knows that keeping the commandments is for our own good and will make us happy, yet He loves freedom and liberty so much, He will not force our will, even if it is for our own good. "If you want to," He says, "if you're motivated by love, then I would like to show you the way to happiness through obedience to My commandments." There is no force, only love.

The United States of America came into existence partly because people wanted to choose. In Europe, it was the king or the ruling class who decided what you must do or not do. The lack of liberty compelled people to leave and prompted the birth of freedom in our fair land. "But," people may argue, "the infractions back in those days were big-time interference in people's lives." And that's true. It was major trampling of their rights, but do we do this to others in a small-time manner today? And if we do it in the little matters, what's to stop us from pressing on to the "big" matters? I hope we can see this as it really is, for in our wisdom we think we see it all so clearly, and it is so easy for us to define duty for someone else. When we do this, we violate the spirit of liberty, and liberty is a key element to the government of God, not just in heaven, but here on this earth.

In contrast to the spirit of liberty, there is the mark of Cain. The mark of Cain is the spirit of control, of commanding, and ruling over others. The mark of Cain compels; it uses force, pressure, persecution, and intimidation. Let's look at how it worked in the life of the one for whom it was named.

Cain was the first-born son of Adam and Eve. The Bible says his chosen occupation was as a tiller of ground. In this he followed his parents' example; they had kept the Garden at God's own command. Both he and his younger brother Abel had been instructed by their parents in the worship of God, and both were members of the first "church." But being members of that first family and knowing all about the worship of God, even having been taught by those who had seen God face-to-face, was not sufficient in Cain's experience. Oh, yes, Cain had religion, but Abel had the Spirit of the Lord, and there's a big difference.

Cain had not outwardly rejected the worship of God. He built an altar just as his brother did. Cain also obeyed the command of God to bring a sacrifice, but instead of a lamb, the symbol of Christ's death for his transgressions, Cain brought the works of his own hands, the produce of his fields. Don't be so quick to write off Cain's religious experience as nonexistent. Cain heard the voice of God speaking to him, something an awful lot of Christians tell me they never experience. It is at this point that so many miss the underlying issues in the story and look only at the outward disobedience. Let's look at the attitudes of the heart and see whether we can't bring this story a little closer to home.

Cain and Abel were of the same religion, same church, and the same family. The truths that lie ahead of us deal more with our relationships and how we relate in our own groups and churches and among friends than with other churches and denominations. For if we cannot relate well among ourselves, what hope do we have of sharing the "good news" with others?

What do we do when someone sees his or her duty to God differently from how I do? Genesis 4:8 shares that after Cain's offering was rejected and Abel's accepted, "Cain *talked* with Abel his brother" (emphasis supplied). Imagine the scene. Do you see some force, some compelling in Cain's attitude, as he "talked" with his brother? Do you see his indignation and temper rising when Abel won't see it his way? Cain wanted his brother's sympathy. He wanted Abel to agree with him about how unfair it was that God wouldn't accept his offering, but Abel wouldn't, and indeed couldn't, agree with such a sentiment. He was quite willing to let Cain do whatever he wanted, but he dared not join him in his choice. When Cain could not force Abel to side with him, he "rose up . . . and slew him."

Today in the church, in all the churches, there is an epidemic of such violence. No, we don't literally slay our brothers and sisters. We don't have to! We slay them with the tongue. We talk about them, destroy their reputations, spread gossip, and are just as murderous in our sphere of influence as was Cain so long ago. We do these things because we don't agree with them or they with us, and we set out to destroy them precisely because we can't control them. If they don't see things our way, then we manifest this attitude of control or force or destruction because self can't have its own way.

One Bible commentary says, "Any man, be he minister or layman, who seeks to compel or control the reason of any other man, becomes an agent of Satan, to do his work, and in the sight of the heavenly universe he bears the mark of Cain" (1:1087). How many of us, if we could see as God does, would find ourselves wearing the mark of Cain, all because of our attitude of control and manipulation when it comes to others? We must remember that bigoted religionists trying to force others to see things their way and to act according to their dictates have committed the most terrible atrocities, both in the past and in the present.

It wasn't long ago that I flew to Ireland, and you know what is going on in that country. There are Protestant Christians who refuse to give the Catholic population the right to follow their own choices when it comes to the manner in which they worship and perceive God. I think we can all agree that it isn't right. Everyone has the God-given right to worship as he or she sees fit or even to not worship at all.

Now let's look at the Catholics in Ireland. Do you suppose they give the Protestants the right to worship as they see fit? Not on your life. I was there; I saw the bombings and the shattered lives in their aftermath. They both claim to be Christian, and both groups ought to be ashamed. They have made religion into a blight and a curse upon the earth. If you were to view such actions objectively, you would be forgiven the impulse to throw up your hands in disgust, before discarding both religions as unworthy of the name.

Let's move a little southwestward to the nation of Israel, and what do we have? Israelis and Palestinians share a common history and revere many of the same religious sites while engaged in a battle that involves massacre, assassinations, terrorist tactics, and a woeful disregard for civilian population. All the while, the Jews are fighting what they believe is a battle for their existence as a religion and a nation, and the Palestinians think of it as a holy war for their religion. If you were to visit the people on either side of this conflict, you would think of them as civilized and pleasant, but a history of religious bigotry and racial persecution has left both groups with enough bitterness and hatred to last for generations.

So the world looks on and is revolted by the scene before them. Diplomats try time and time again to bring peace, only to find that peace is an elusive thing for those who would be religious revolutionaries or any whose worldview consists primarily of the idea that those with whom we disagree must be treated as enemies. The remains of Yugoslavia have disintegrated into terrible chaos of ethnic and religious persecution, the likes of which have not been witnessed in Europe since the days of the Third Reich. Ethnic and religious purity inspires men who claim to be religious to torture, murder, and rape on such a scale that Bosnia and Serbia have become synonymous with evil. It's all done in the name of religion.

Just a few years back hundreds of thousands died when members of the Hutu and Tutsi tribes in Africa started killing one another. As the news erupted about the mass of deaths, the world stood horrified at the thought of Christians killing Christians. Would you want anything to do with their religions? No, not the way they practice them. The Bible says it is by their fruits that you shall know them. You can go on and on naming example after example with your only limitation being your willingness to turn musty old pages of history. The mark of Cain has been alive and well, even though its namesake is long dead. The question we must ask ourselves is, "Has it been living in my heart as well?"

Are the happenings out in the world really all that different from what is going on in our own church? When someone in our congregation doesn't see things our way, and we start gossiping and tearing down, aren't those assaults very similar to the hatred manifest in Ireland? What about independent ministries and their attacks on the church? Do you see the spirit of Cain? I do! I wouldn't want to attend meetings sponsored by some of these organizations. What about our church and its leadership? Do you see the mark of Cain manifested toward those same independent ministries? Have you seen it toward those who would use our denominational name? Friends, the attitude of religious bigotry exists today within our very own churches. Would you view someone suspiciously because he or she attended an independent meeting? I've been at meetings with various independent ministries. They can't get along with one another. They are at one another's throats, and they're busy throwing one another out. Why is it so hard to see that the question is not whether one is in or out of the organized church? The mark of Cain is the real problem, and it continually yields a harvest of strife and discord.

Once a man came up to me and said, "I've got to study all the theological positions of these different ministries, so I can decide who is right."

"No you don't!" I urged him. "Just look at their fruit. If it's bad, run from their theology." I'm not saying we shouldn't have correct theology, but there is many a man out there espousing correct theology who doesn't know the first thing about heart religion or the transforming power of Christ in the life. They are religious zealots pushing their agenda, and God help anyone who gets in their way, for this type of individual is the very embodiment of the mark of Cain.

First Corinthians 3:3 says, "For ye are yet carnal: for whereas there is among you envying, and strife, and divisions, are ye not carnal, and walk as men?" Paul, under inspiration of God, says that if there are envying, strife, and divisions in our church, it is because we are still carnal. Do you think that God views the contention between the various ministries and the church any differently from how He did in Paul's day? The next verse states, "For while one saith, I am of Paul; and another, I am of Apollos; are ye not carnal?" When we are fighting among ourselves, Satan smiles for he knows he has us. Another author wrote on this theme, sharing, it seems, the very words of Satan as he spoke with his imps. " 'We must cause distraction and division. We must destroy their anxiety for their own souls, and lead them to criticise, to judge, and to accuse and condemn one another, and to cherish selfishness and enmity. For these sins, God banished us from his presence; and all who follow our example will meet a similar fate' " (*The Spirit of Prophecy,* 4:340).

We have been playing the devil's game, and it is time we woke up to the error of our ways.

Galatians 5 talks about the fruits of the Spirit, saying they are "love, joy, peace, longsuffering, gentleness, goodness, faith, meekness" (verses 22, 23). I have to ask myself, "Has my attitude been one of love toward others with whom I disagree?" Do we have a spirit of joy about us?

I was at a meeting once and a man was going to get up and preach. His disposition was so sour that just his expression would have stopped a charging rhino. It is not wrong to ask ourselves how we are to relate to the turmoil and conflict in the church these days and how much of a responsibility we bear. You can be sure your non-Christian neighbors are watching how we relate to others in our churches, and they are drawing conclusions about whether we are really tasting of God's peace or not.

Am I longsuffering toward those with whom I may not see things eye to eye? Am I gentle, and is my spirit meek? Or does my life manifest the works of the flesh Paul speaks of in the preceding verses, such as hatred, variance (disagreement, quarrel, or dispute), emulations (trying to equal or surpass people), wrath, strife, envyings, and murders? God must think this is serious because He says, "They which do such things shall not inherit the kingdom of God" (verse 21).

If your theology is not producing the fruits of the Spirit in your life, be very careful about your theology. If your attendance at church, an independent ministry meeting, or even a home worship group is not moving you toward this experience, then you need to be careful about your attendance. Does this make me antichurch? Not in the least! But no matter what your view of whom and what the church is, it had better be advancing your spiritual walk or you are wasting your time and energy.

If we are manifesting a critical spirit; if we love controversy; if we desire to control others; and if in the exercise of our criticism, controversy, and attempted control we are thwarted and become angry, then we have become partakers in the mark of Cain. "And Cain was very wroth, and his countenance fell" (Genesis 4:5). "God gives to every soul freedom to think, and to follow his own convictions…. In all matters where principle is involved, 'let every man be fully persuaded in his own mind.' Rom. 14:12, 5. In Christ's kingdom there is no lordly oppression, no compulsion of manner" (*The Desire of Ages*, 550, 551).

For many a century, the issue facing true Christians was the use of force to control others. The history of religious persecution has always been the history of "good" people using the most inhuman tortures and penalties to try and force others to be good too! Most of us believe that to one degree or another this issue of control and force will become "the issue" in the last days, and yet we have apparently been very slow to learn the lesson ourselves. Is it really that different to forbid one to buy and sell unless you receive a mark, a sign of allegiance, than it is to forbid one to preach or speak unless they adhere to certain restrictions to prove their loyalty to the organization apart from any biblical standard?

If we are in the habit of acting in this manner, it will be perfectly natural for us to join with the oppressors at the end of time, for in little ways and in little actions we have been acting just like they will act. Only those who understand the value of liberty, as God does, will grant its benefits to others. What a debt of gratitude we owe to those of old who understood the principles so much better than we seem to today.

In the year 1521, the greatest minds and most famous men of the age assembled to hear the objections of a single monk named Martin Luther. Those who opposed Luther knew they could not withstand him in an open and free debate; for truth and the Spirit of God were on his side. Therefore, they took him and had him led through the streets to the meeting place and kept him waiting all day so that he would become impatient. They used the force of their office to manipulate circumstances and make things unpleasant for him. They knew they had to get Martin Luther angry and frustrated if they were to overthrow him, so they did everything possible to tempt him to impatience.

I wonder how we would react to that kind of situation. If someone keeps me waiting for ten minutes, I start getting antsy. Praise God, Luther chose to remain surrendered, and when at last he was called before the assembly, he refused to renounce his positions unless shown his error from the Word of God or from reasonable arguments. He stood alone, one man against the world, and there he uttered words that still thrill us today with their power and import: "Here I stand. I can do no other. May God help me."

Luther had no way of knowing, but he had taken the first steps in bringing religious liberty to the world. Six years later the empire was fully divided on the question of religion. Protestantism had taken root in Germany, and the state church was determined to see it destroyed, but the men who held it dear were too committed and fearless to be swayed by mere threats. A compromise was offered suggesting that those areas that had already accepted Luther's teaching be allowed liberty to continue in their course, while forbidding the spread of Protestantism beyond their boundaries.

" 'The Lutheran princes were guaranteed the free exercise of their religion. . . . Happily they looked at the principle on which this arrangement was based, and they acted in faith. What was that principle? It was the right of Rome to coerce conscience and forbid free inquiry' " (*The Great Controversy*, 200). " 'Let us reject this decree,' said the princes. 'In matters of conscience the majority has no power.' . . . To protect liberty of conscience is the duty of the state, and this is the limit of its authority in matters of religion" (Ibid., 201).

"The protesters had moreover affirmed their right to utter freely their convictions of truth. They would not only believe and obey, but teach what the word of God presents, and they denied the right of priest or magistrate to interfere. The Protest of Spires was a solemn witness against religious intolerance, and the assertion of the right of all men to worship God according to the dictates of their own consciences" (Ibid., 204).

Under the influence of the Spirit of God, these men risked their kingdoms and their lives to defend the right of all to worship God according to their individual convictions. I believe it is time for us, under that same influence, to take the risk of being misunderstood, to take the risk of having friends reject us, even chancing the displeasure of the church, if need be, to defend the rights of all to worship God without being coerced by the majority. I'm not talking about allowing just any doctrine or practice to exist in the church, but rather that we grant everyone the freedom to disagree with our view and still manifest toward them, not just tolerance but the same inspired love that God provides us, as we grow and change. It is time for a rebirth of freedom in our own churches. May religious liberty become not just a revered concept, but also an active principle in all our dealings with our fellow believers regardless of their persuasion. The question is ever before us. Which shall we display to the world, the Spirit of the Lord, or the mark of Cain?

How can we tell? There are four crucial tests to determining which spirit motivates our actions:

1. **A critical spirit.**

   Do I have a disposition to hurt and destroy those who disagree with my ideas? After all, it isn't a question of whether they are attacking me, is it? If we both partake of the same wrong spirit, we simply travel down the winding road to perdition together. As a bumper sticker once said, "Raising Hell Only Lowers Yourself."

2. **A controversial spirit.**

Jesus was surrounded by controversy, which we have examined in this book, yet He never entered into the controversies swirling about Him in spite of repeated attempts to draw Him in. Error cannot be overcome by attack. Truth is its own best defense; it can always stand up to the closest scrutiny. If I find myself constantly in controversy, and always seem to be doing battle for the Lord, perhaps there is a need to examine the spirit I hold. I have known people who were just like steel jaws of a trap, just waiting for the slightest controversy as an excuse to jump into the fray. Remember, the best way to confront error is to live the truth.

3. **A compelling spirit.**

The use of force, whether physical, emotional, political, or economic, to compel another into a religious practice or belief lies at the foundation of Satan's kingdom. All who practice it are doing his work, no matter how lofty their ambitions. The world tried to force Martin Luther to change his position, yet he claimed in the face of all their pressure: "'Unless therefore I am convinced by the testimony of Scripture or by the clearest reasoning . . . *I cannot and will not retract,* for it is unsafe for a Christian to speak against his conscience'" (*The Great Controversy*, 160, italics in the original). If we violate this principle of another's free conscience in word or action, we have a spirit of compelling. I've known some church members who refuse to speak to someone they feel is doing wrong. In most cases, this makes life more pleasant for the one being shunned, but it does reveal the spirit that motivates the heart. If we use phrases such as, "Brother, I'll grant you that point, but not in this church," or "This is the way we have always done it and always will," or "I must insist that you adhere to church policy," or even, "Here, we go by majority vote." If any of these phrases or similar verbiage is coming from your mouth, know with certainty what spirit you have.

4. **A spirit of control.**

   Control is the culmination of the other attitudes. Cain rose up against his brother Abel and slew him. This spirit is the "my way and my way now" attitude, and you can see it in the world, in business, in unions, in government, in politics, and, yes, friend, you can see it in the church. In Christ's day this was happening in the church. "Howbeit no man spake openly of him for fear of the Jews" (John 7:13). They were intimidated, and too often in our day people place restrictions on others, even other ministers, telling them where and how they should work, even what they should say, using the power and influence of their offices to intimidate those under them. This is contrary to the freedom God desires wherein He controls all the laborers. Let us beware of placing restrictions where God places none. No human being should seek to control another or to dictate to them their duty before God. Everyone must keep their dependence upon God and not their fellow laborer, no matter how highly esteemed they may be.

So when you see these marks—criticism, controversy, compelling, and control—run for your life, for you have met the enemy, and in many cases he may be the person looking back at you from the mirror. Throughout the history of the church, the "good" have always persecuted the righteous. Your actions now will determine which of these two groups you are preparing to join in the final days of this earth's history.

CHAPTER 4

TINKERING, MEDDLING, AND PRESCRIBING

"It is an honour for a man to cease from strife: but every fool will be meddling" (Proverbs 20:3).

Would you like to eliminate two-thirds of the problems in your friendships, churches, and institutions? Sure, you would! All of us would, or would we? There is a statement found in *Testimonies for the Church*, volume 2, page 466, that states, "Two thirds of all the church trials arise from this source." The author is, of course, speaking of gossip, but it has been my experience that we as a people do not understand gossip for what it is. This "source" is what I call tinkering, meddling, and prescribing. All too often, because we are not involved in what our preconceived idea of gossip is, we do not realize what we are doing, and then we wonder why we have problems. So allow me to share some biblical examples of these mischief-makers at work.

In John 21, we are shown one of those scenes of Jesus and His disciples that I love so well. The Crucifixion and Resurrection morning are past, and they are once again in Galilee. Morning sunlight plays among the waves, making them sparkle, while the hillsides burst forth in the green garb of spring, and the air is filled with the scent of flowers and the songs of birds. It is in this peaceful setting, along that distant shore, that Christ and Peter take a walk. Here at last, the Savior of the world confronts the very one who denied Him. Why? Because the Lord in His tender mercy knows that for Peter's sake, this issue must be laid to rest.

After answering Christ's queries into his commitment to Him three times, Peter declares earnestly, "Lord, thou knowest all things; thou knowest that I love thee" (verse 17). It is the emotional high point between Christ and Peter, and he knows that the fellowship between them is restored, and Jesus once more invites him to "Follow me" (verse 19).

Then Peter, glancing behind them, notices John following after them, and somehow he can't resist tinkering, just a little. In verse 21 he asks Jesus, "Lord, and what shall this man do?"

Peter had an inquiring mind. He wanted to know what John was to do. What were his duties? What were his obligations to be? "What will You assign this man to do?" Curiosity is normal, I suppose, but what do you think Jesus thought about this? Before we look at the answer, ask yourself, have I ever been involved in this type of behavior?

"Jesus saith unto him, If I will that he tarry till I come, what is that to thee? follow thou me."

Jesus was really blunt here. He basically told him, it's none of your business what I'm going to do with John. Your work, Peter, is to follow Me. We know, looking back at history, that Jesus had a special work for both these men to perform, but it was not the same work, and it was not Peter's job to be tinkering in John's business.

As we look at Peter's character and his weaknesses, it seems obvious that Peter had his hands full just taking care of himself. How often are you and I like him, inquiring into the affairs of others, when our attention should be upon the formation of our own characters. "How many today are like Peter! They are interested in the affairs of others, and anxious to know their duty, while they are in danger of neglecting their own" (*The Desire of Ages*, 816).

Surely we wouldn't neglect our duty, but do we have an abiding experience with Christ? Are we allowing Him to guide and direct our lives every moment of every day? Is my marriage after Heaven's order? Is my home one where angels delight to linger? Are my children learning to love God and make Him a practical part of their lives? Are we fulfilling our duties in our own lives and homes? If not, then perhaps we, like Peter, should find our hands too busy with the task at hand to spend time inspecting the duties of our fellow Christians. "It is the duty of everyone to follow Christ, without undue anxiety as to the work assigned to others" (Ibid.).

Tinkering never ends with just tinkering. It always moves on to meddling. We find an example of such meddling in Luke 10. Jesus was visiting in the home of Mary and Martha. Mary sat at Jesus' feet and listened intently to His words, but Martha was encumbered with serving the meal and came to Him and said, "Lord, dost thou not care that my sister hath left me to serve alone?" (verse 40).

Do you see what's happening? Martha is burdened, and she lays out her complaint almost accusatorily to Jesus. Then when Jesus doesn't immediately act as she thinks He should, she moves straight into meddling with her sister. "Bid her therefore that she help me" (verse 40).

"And Jesus answered and said unto her, Martha, Martha, thou art careful and troubled about many things: But one thing is needful: and Mary hath chosen that good part, which shall not be taken away from her" (verses 41, 42).

Martha was meddling in the affairs of Mary. Her motives were pure, and she was trying to be helpful, but she was not acting under the guidance of the Spirit of God. So many of us are, like Martha, meddling in the affairs of our fellow brothers and sisters. And it's a recipe for disaster in our relationships and friendships with others. It's our job to take the other person, whoever they may be, before Christ with sincere prayers and then leave them there and allow God to direct them in the way He sees best.

Does it really seem possible that we could be meddling in the affairs of others that much? I believe we are. I believe we are seriously involved in the affairs of others. In fact, I believe we are so wrapped up in the inner workings of other people's lives, or the church's work, or this or that ministry's work that we are fearfully neglecting what should be our first work—preparing our own souls. The devil knows this, and he does all in his power to encourage meddling, and when the time is right he urges us to move on from meddling to prescribing.

Mark 9:38-40 shows what happens when we move on to prescribing for others. As we pick up the story, John is speaking to Jesus. "Master, we saw one casting out devils in thy name, and he followeth not us: and we forbad him, because he followeth not us." Do you see what's going on here? They see this fellow casting out devils, and he isn't following the disciples; he isn't part of their group, and yet he has the nerve to be casting out devils in Christ's name. The disciples didn't want that, so they forbade him. Today we might say, "He followeth not the church, or he doesn't support this ministry. He didn't graduate from one of our colleges, and he doesn't even have the approval of the conference committee." Jesus, as He did so often in the disciples' experience, disagreed with their reasoning, and perhaps if He were here today He would disagree with our reasoning, too, because this is how He responded:

"Forbid him not: for there is no man which shall do a miracle in my name, that can lightly speak evil of me. For he that is not against us is on our part."

Why did He say that? Christ wasn't fooled by what was going on. His Spirit was leading this other fellow, and the disciples needed to take their hands off the controls, and so do we. God is still quite capable of taking care of His own work. We had better let Him control the work, lest we find ourselves working against Him. It is faithlessness in God that leads men to put forth their own puny efforts to try and save the church from this or that danger. The moment we stretch out our hands to steady the ark and attempt to use our authority in God's sphere, we publicly confess our lack of faith, admitting that we must do for God what He seems incapable of doing for Himself. It is only through the mercy of God that more have not suffered the fate of Uzzah.

The spirit of control is prevalent today. There is the spirit of ruling or governing, of domination, or acting as conscience or Holy Spirit, over our friends, over the work in the church, or ministries, or over institutions, and this has to leave our experience. "In matters of conscience the soul must be left untrammeled. No one is to control another's mind, to judge for another, or to prescribe his duty" (*The Desire of Ages,* 550).

My grandmother used to have a name for people who did such things; she called them busybodies. What does a busybody do? Well, there are probably thousands of different variations, but every one of them has some of the following elements in common. We assess what you should or shouldn't do. Then we compel you to follow us. If we can't do that, we set out to convince others of your inappropriate ways. Let me give you a few examples.

When Sally and I decided to sell our business and our huge log home, we were motivated by a vision, a goal if you will, of really coming to know God in a way we hadn't found Him to that point in our lives. We couldn't even fully explain it, but we knew God wanted us to move to the wilderness. How do you suppose our fellow church members reacted? Do you think they said, "Go for it, Jim, we're behind you. You can do it! We think that's great!" No, the talk started going around. "They're going to hide in a cave. They've gone fanatical. They're going to lose their talents. Are they crazy? How can they give up a place like the one they own?" I don't think there was one person who came to us and encouraged us. They thought we were crazy, but they didn't just keep it to themselves. They talked and tinkered until Sally and I became aware of a cool reserve seeping into our friendships. During our last few weeks there, we could just feel the eyes of our fellow church members following us, boring into us. It was as if everyone wanted to see for himself what sort of lunatics we were.

We had no idea at the time that God was taking us out to teach us something so that we could then be used of Him to reach others. We only see that in hindsight, and certainly we couldn't explain it then to those dear people at church. I want to make it clear that we don't look down on those people. Had the situation been reversed, we could easily have done just what they did. And we love them still. But that doesn't alter the fact that they were tinkering and meddling.

In the wilderness we found an experience with God, and as we started to share what we found, we made a number of special friendships, but perhaps none so special or so dear as the one with the Waters family. When we first started preaching, there were a number of different families that wanted to join together with us in a ministry. There were also some institutions that wanted us to join with them, but we'd pray about it, and we just couldn't get comfortable with the idea. After much soul searching and seeking God, we felt strongly that the Lord wanted us to join together and form a ministry with the Waters family. Well, a number of our friends in the wilderness were getting together for a picnic, including some who had wanted to join with us. Most of these families had never met the Waters family and were eager to get a chance to see these people that the Hohnbergers planned to join efforts with. Many of these families were quite conservative, and they were scandalized because Alane showed up for the picnic wearing red pants and a Mexican top. Even worse than that, she brought hydrogenated peanut butter, and the talk just went wild. "Do you see who the Hohnbergers are going to associate with? She wore pants! Can you believe it—pants! They eat hydrogenated peanut butter! I would have thought the Hohnbergers would have at least picked someone conservative to form a ministry with." Tinkering and meddling flourished. These people were shocked, but we didn't care about the red pants or peanut butter; we had been looking at their hearts, and that was what attracted us to them. In Tom and Alane Waters, we had seen a clear reflection of our own desire to serve God with all our heart and teach our children to do likewise. That's the way God looks at us. He sees the desires of the heart, but man looks at the outward appearance.

Those people didn't just content themselves to talk about it in Montana. It spread to several states. Everyone seemed to have something to say about these people the Hohnbergers were going to join up with. Now, my wife didn't wear red pants, and she had advanced our diet to the point that we used "natural" peanut butter instead of the hydrogenated variety. But we never said a word to Alane about her red pants or her peanut butter, and if you were to see Alane today, it is doubtful you'll see her in red pants. If you eat at her table, you won't find hydrogenated peanut butter. And yet, there were many people who were willing to judge her on these nonmoral issues and take away her liberty to be led by God in His own timing. We laugh over these stories, but in truth it was kind of sad. It hurt Sally and me because we knew what we saw in them—two people who were in love with God and committed to serving Him.

When my son Matthew was getting ready to set up his wilderness real estate practice, he needed a car. So I went to a car dealer I had done business with before and told him, "God told me to come to you. He said you would find just what I want." The man looked at me in disbelief, but I continued. "This is what I'm looking for. We need a four-wheel-drive vehicle that an old grandma has driven. It's got to have very low mileage and be in perfect condition, and we want it for about five thousand dollars."

The man, I'll just call him Jay, looked at me doubtfully and said, "Jim, we don't get many of those kinds of cars in, and when we do, it's only every four or five years."

"Don't worry about it, Jay. The Lord will bring it to you. Call me when it comes in."

Three weeks later Jay called me up. "Jim, I don't believe it! This eighty-year-old woman drove in. She had a Subaru that she's owned for years. It has only fifty thousand miles on it, and it looks like it just came off the showroom floor. Best of all, I can sell it to you for four thousand, nine hundred dollars."

I said, "Bring it up. We'll take it!" God chose the vehicle for my son, and yet, there were families that started saying I was cruel to my son because a teenage boy should have a truck that's high-lifted and has fast gears. Of course, the gossip got back to my son. They were trying to make him feel deprived because his father was "forcing" him into a vehicle that was too mature.

Some people have come to my boys and told them, "It's not right that your parents don't allow you to have any dogs, cats, or horses." And it's true; we don't have any of those pets, not because we don't like them, but because we decided early on after moving to the wilderness that we wanted to make friends with the wildlife. My boys have had all kinds of wild pets, from squirrels to wild deer they can touch and hand feed. We had the blessed opportunity to tame a black bear. He'd even play on the swing set with my boys and still, with all those special experiences that very few children will ever have, there are those who would like to try and make them feel bad because they don't have a dog like other kids.

My wife often travels and shares what she has learned about homeschooling with others. During one lecture, it was ninety-five degrees and the humidity was almost one hundred percent, and it is even hotter for the speaker on the stage under the lights. She wore a dress that had three-quarter length sleeves and didn't bother with tights, but just wore socks and shoes. Would you believe that because someone saw a little bit of calf when she stepped up to the platform, news quickly spread through the meeting that Sally dressed immodestly.

Another time some well-meaning folks were embarrassed because of my eating habits. Normally I eat two meals a day, which was very acceptable to them, but when I'm out speaking I eat three meals. The reason is that I eat lightly in the morning so my mind will be clear, and I do the same at lunch. By evening, with the stress of speaking all day and the lighter than normal meals, my blood sugar crashes and I'm starved. On this particular occasion, I ate an apple and a piece of bread to give my body a boost. Well, a man came up to me and told me I was a disgrace to the message because I was eating three meals instead of two. I tried to explain to him the problem I faced on weekends, but he was dogmatic in his determination that I should set a proper example for all the other men. If I had to eat, he asserted I should go hide in my room. Although the man was sincere and thought he was doing me and God a favor, it shows the casual disregard we have for the feelings and needs of others as we pursue our own agendas.

Jesus Christ had to endure more tinkering, meddling, and prescribing than any person who ever lived on this earth. Even His parents and siblings criticized His actions. In fact, one of the few who ever gave a correct evaluation of Him was the Roman governor Pilate, who said, "I find in him no fault at all" (John 18:38).

Nevertheless, the Jewish leaders meddled constantly. This Man eats with publicans, harlots, and sinners. This Man is from Nazareth. How knoweth this Man letters, having never learned? This guy didn't attend our school system or our seminary. He was homeschooled, and obviously He doesn't know about keeping Himself pure, because He preaches to Samaritans and Gentiles!

We look disdainfully upon the Jewish leaders, but I believe I can safely say that every one of us has been guilty of this practice with our friends or family. We may not murder them, but in putting down others we make ourselves feel better, and in so feeding on their faults, we are distracted from our own. In many ways we are like a flock of chickens when a new one is introduced. All the others gather around and start pecking at it. We pick one another apart like a flock of underfed vultures. "We think with horror of the cannibal who feasts on the still warm and trembling flesh of his victim; but are the results of even this practice more terrible than are the agony and ruin caused by misrepresenting motive, blackening reputation, dissecting character?" (*Education*, 235).

Some may be vegetarians in name, but many of us are still cannibals in practice. As Proverbs 18:21 states, "Death and life are in the power of the tongue: and they that love it shall eat the fruit thereof." "In Scripture, backbiters are classed with 'haters of God,' with 'inventors of evil things,' with those who are 'without natural affection, implacable, unmerciful,' 'full of envy, murder, debate, deceit, malignity.' It is 'the judgment of God, that they which commit such things are worthy of death.' Romans 1:30, 31, 29, 32. He whom God accounts a citizen of Zion is he that 'speaketh the truth in his heart;' 'that backbiteth not with his tongue,' 'nor taketh up a reproach against his neighbor.' Psalm 15:2, 3. . . .

"Closely allied to gossip is the covert insinuation, the sly innuendo, by which the unclean in heart seek to insinuate the evil they dare not openly express" (*Education*, 235, 236). "Seest thou a man that is hasty in his words? there is more hope of a fool than of him" (Proverbs 29:20). Can God explain it any more clearly to us? "In one moment, by the hasty, passionate, careless tongue, may be wrought evil that a whole lifetime's repentance cannot undo" (*Education*, 236, 237).

The men who formed the laws and principles for founding our nation had experienced tinkering, meddling, and prescribing from the ruling class in Europe to such an extent that they were determined that it should never happen again. In our Declaration of Independence was written, "We hold these truths to be self-evident, that all men are created equal, that they are endowed by their Creator, with certain inalienable Rights, that among these are Life, Liberty and the pursuit of Happiness." They felt strongly about the freedom of the individual. Patrick Henry stated the case so strongly that it still shocks me today to hear his words. "Give me liberty, or give me death!" How many in our churches still long for freedom and would echo his words? How many truly feel, as I do, that they'd rather be in the grave than to have others messing with what kind of vehicle my son should drive, how long my wife's dresses should be, whether I should go to Montana, to whom I should preach, or what type of peanut butter my friends can eat? Give me death, before you do this to me. It's miserable, friend, yet this is what we do to one another. We are either going to give one another liberty in these areas or we are going to give one another death.

Why do we have this preoccupation with the supposed defects and faults of others? *Sons and Daughters of God,* page 348, explains it. "The truly converted man has no inclination to think or talk of the faults of others." Do you know whom that rebukes? Me! Shame on me! I need to go deeper with God. "True Christians will not exult in exposing the faults and deficiencies of others. . . . To the Christian every act of faultfinding, every word of censure or condemnation, is painful" (*Testimonies for the Church,* 5:96).

"He that covereth a transgression seeketh love; but he that repeateth a matter separateth very friends" (Proverbs 17:9). Oh, how often have I seen this demonstrated! It is out of the abundance of the heart that the mouth speaketh. When I was a little lad and went to the old family doctor, the very first thing he did was to have me stick out my tongue so he could look in my mouth. He could tell an awful lot about my health with just that one look. God is the same way. He says, let me see what your tongue has been doing and I'll know the condition of your heart.

So, how do we change these long-established patterns of behavior? First must come the realization that with men this is impossible, but with God all things are possible. Hence, we will only succeed as we prayerfully depend upon divine guidance. The following steps are intended only to provide practical options and in no way are a substitute for heavenly impressions upon the mind willing to respond. They do, however, provide Christ-centered principles on which we can focus.

The first principle is embodied in a question that I always have to ask myself before I open my mouth. Do I, at this moment, have God's permission to tinker, meddle, or prescribe in this person's life, or in this ministry's business, or in this church's affairs? Even if I do see faults, it doesn't mean I automatically have the right to correct them. Christ Himself told His disciples that there were many things He wished to tell them, but they were not prepared to receive them. Only God knows the heart. You and I don't. If I feel inclined to speak out about something, I stop to see whether it is God asking me to do so, or if it is simply my flesh rising within me. One of the best tests I have found is to question my motive. Is it for the purpose of restoration, sympathy, and compassion that I want to speak up, or is it envy, jealousy, or pride? If we would honestly answer these questions, the vast majority of our interpersonal problems in the church would go away instantly, because 90 percent of the time we would keep our mouths shut!

The second principle will deal with 8 percent of what remains. Do I, right now, have this person's *permission* to say what I am going to share? To force unwanted instruction on an unwilling recipient is not of God. I have to deal with wives dragging their unwilling husbands along for counseling. You can just see the triumph in their body language as they expectantly wait for me to "straighten out" their erring partner. I wish you could sit in on such a counseling session, because the results are not the expected ones. The husband has not given me permission to deal with his problems, so I deal only with the wife's, much to her surprise! A burning flax shall ye not quench, the Bible tells us, and if we would inquire of God more often He would tell us, "Leave this man alone. I am working with this man. Leave him to Me. Encourage him in the walk." Too often we can extinguish the last spark of hope with our "good intentions." The gospel never forces people, and neither must we! In most cases when the men see that I'm not out to get them, they give permission to go ahead. They actually want help, but first they have to see a pure motive and a respectful approach.

Last, but not least, the final 2 percent we have to deal with is to be sensitive to the changing situation. Even if God and the individual give you permission to speak, one or both may withdraw that permission as you go along and then you *must* stop. This is hard to do because we have our carefully laid-out points, and we want to get to them so they aren't wasted. But too many of us want to beat a dead horse. I was counseling with a man once, who had asked me to tell him some things about himself, but just as I was getting going he said, "Enough, enough. I get the idea." So I stopped. He had enough to work on with just a little bit. Don't discourage another. Ever keep in mind that you are dealing with a soul that God died for, and they are infinitely precious in the sight of Heaven. Sometimes this withdrawal of permission is not audible, but you can just sense they are closing up. Check with the Lord. Be sensitive to them and treat them as you would like to be treated if the roles were reversed.

Let me share Ernie's story and see whether you can't relate to him. Ernie was one of those kids born athletic. He loved sports by temperament and through his father's training. He was also a professed Christian, and while he knew that there were some problems relating to Christianity and competition, it had not yet become an issue between the Lord and him.

Then one day he heard a sermon in church that dealt with this issue. It was not dogmatic but pointed out the difficulties in maintaining a Christian spirit while trying to be competitive. If he had been left alone there is no way of knowing what influence, if any, the day's message might have brought about. But no one will ever know because a zealous member of the congregation came up to him after the sermon and confronted him like this. "So, Ernie, old boy, in light of the message the pastor brought to us this morning, what do you plan to do with your competitive sports?"

He didn't plan to do anything at that moment, but this experience unquestionably made him reluctant to do anything in the future either. It also caused him to feel persecuted and helped prepare the way for him to join in a fringe movement that soon came along. Before too long he believed that church organization is evil and left the church. Oh, what an influence our words have for good or for evil! Only in eternity will we be able to judge the effect of our tinkering, meddling, and prescribing. By God's grace may the record we someday face be one we will not be ashamed for all to see.

In closing, I give you permission to tinker, meddle, and prescribe in your *own* life under the guidance of God. There is nothing we do that so tells the world about our connection with God or a lack thereof as do our words. "For by thy words thou shalt be justified, and by thy words thou shalt be condemned" (Matthew 12:37).

CHAPTER 5

PLEASE UNDERSTAND ME

"Let love be without dissimulation.... Be kindly affectioned
one to another with brotherly love; in honour preferring one another"
(Romans 12:9, 10).

Do you think it is possible for two very close friends to misunderstand each other and to hold totally different views of the same issue? Can two close families find themselves completely and totally on different sides of a conflict even when heretofore they have been closely united? I think, in fact I know, they can, and when it occurs, each party sees things from their perspective as black and white, as right and wrong. Both are honest and sincere in their views and yet wonder why the other cannot see it as they do.

Have you ever had this experience? How many of you reading these words feel misunderstood by a friend, a parent, a child, or a spouse? I'm pretty sure your answer is "Yes." As I have spoken all over the world, I have asked this question to countless crowds of people, and nearly every hand is raised in response. I can authoritatively affirm there are an awful lot of misunderstandings among us as Christians.

In our desire to seek God and to be one with Him, many times we have injured and wounded one another. I have done it, and I'm sure you have done it too. Unless we learn to hear what the other is saying with a listening heart and not just a listening ear, we will continue to go forth with good intentions and alienate those about us, simply because we cannot hear the plea of the human heart to be understood. How can we answer the plea, "Please understand me"? Let's explore the question together.

Ephesians 4:1-3 says, "I therefore, the prisoner of the Lord, beseech you that ye walk worthy of the vocation wherewith ye are called, with all lowliness and meekness, with longsuffering, forbearing one another in love; endeavouring to keep the unity of the Spirit in the bond of peace." "With all lowliness and meekness" is what God says. So, when you and I get together and a point comes up that we don't see eye-to-eye on, I can't come to you with just *some* lowliness and *some* meekness. No! I must have *all* lowliness and meekness. In other words, I must come to you with my self-will dead to its desires and alive only to fulfill the will of God. My job is not to straighten you out but to understand you.

I love to play with children. It is so much fun to play hide and seek with a toddler. Have you ever done that? They go and hide, and as long as they've got their head behind a chair or some other object, they think they are hidden. Is there anything wrong with their reasoning? No, it is perfectly normal for that stage of life. Did you know that is just how it is with many of those who don't see things our way? God may look at them and be satisfied with the understanding they have for their stage of development. The problem is that we are not satisfied! We want everyone to be just like us and at the same stage of development. If everyone were just like me, then the world would be a much better place. Or would it? Maybe not!

The text we just read asks me to use all meekness and understanding, but it doesn't demand I give up my ideas, my views, or my convictions. I may need to die to self, though, and that never hurt anyone. If my self-will is dead I can hear what you have to say from the position of what is best for you rather than what I want the outcome to be.

Romans 12:9 says, "Let love be without dissimulation." Do you know what that means? I didn't, and too often we skip over such texts when the wording is a little different from our vocabulary. If you look it up like I finally did, you'll discover it means to make dissimilar or to become dissimilar. In modern words we might say, "Don't let your love be separated by differences." It goes on in verse 10 to state, "Be kindly affectioned one to another with brotherly love; in honour preferring one another." I love the way the Bible phrases such injunctions. It doesn't say, "If you feel like it," it simply says "Be." Once a friend told me, "It means 'do,' " and I like that, because from God's perspective it is just the way things ought to be. Every Christian should be loving to their brothers and sisters. Jesus Himself commented, "These things I commanded you, that ye love one another" (John 15:17). But to love as God does is a very different thing than to simply know what we should be doing. Have you tried to prefer others' opinions and ideas over and above your own? Let me tell you, it isn't easy. We cannot generate those types of behaviors and actions on our own. No human being can, of himself or herself, love another human being this way.

Although I think in black-and-white terms and think things are either right or wrong (and if they aren't black or white I make sure they are—in a hurry!), the Lord is showing me that through Him I must develop an attitude of understanding toward others. This doesn't mean agreement with them, but that I sincerely attempt to grasp not just their words but what they are really saying, regardless of my opinions and convictions. It's my job to make sure they know in my words, actions, and even my body language that I really care for them.

Some years ago a family visited in our home. These people worked at a religious publishing house, and because they were going to be staying with us for a number of days, they wanted to do something nice for us to say thank you. They brought us some books from their publishing house as gifts. Now, I don't mean just any books. Oh, no. They brought us the best of the best, with nice bindings and brilliant illustrations. When they presented them to us, I could see the excitement on their faces, and I was a little excited too because I enjoy presents, especially if they are unexpected. The books were lovely. Some were study guides, others were true stories, but then I came to *Pilgrim's Progress* by John Bunyan, and I didn't know what to think. This happened soon after we moved to the wilderness, and I had been a Christian for only a few years, so I had never heard of this book. But the title caught my attention. It was a nice book, a hardback with color illustrations. I picked it up and leafed through it, examining some of the illustrations more closely, and, frankly, I was appalled! The images of Christian fighting with the devil were so graphic, it seemed more like science fiction than something edifying. I couldn't believe someone would offer this to me and I trashed it, but not in front of them, of course. I couldn't help wondering how they could think I would want something like that. I was honest and sincere in my judgment, but was I correct? I thought I was.

Thankfully God didn't just let me sit like that in my black-and-white position. He wanted to bring some balance into my life, and He used some friends who visited us later.

"Jim, we have been reading this wonderful book called *Pilgrim's Progress*," Mark told me excitedly. "You have got to read this book!"

I righteously rose up and declared, "Mark, I wouldn't have that book in my home! In fact, some friends tried to give it to me a few weeks ago, and I threw it out!"

"Oh . . . you didn't, Jim!"

"I did!"

"Are you sure that it isn't from God?"

"I'm positive! You should have seen those pictures. I'm sure God wouldn't have anything to do with it."

Mark calmly let me finish. I knew something was up, though, because while I was busy talking, Mark had quietly perused my bookshelves. Finally he found an author he knows I respect and trust in theological matters.

"Do you like this book?" he asked innocently.

"Of course, you know I love that book!" I replied incredulously.

"Do you trust what it says?"

"Mark, I've always believed that God moved that author. You know that." Then he started to read, "In a loathsome dungeon crowded with profligates and felons, John Bunyan breathed the very atmosphere of heaven; and there he wrote his wonderful allegory of the pilgrim's journey from the land of destruction to the celestial city. For over two hundred years that voice from Bedford jail has spoken with thrilling power to the hearts of men."

I sank back into my chair, but Mark kept reading, "Bunyan's *Pilgrim's Progress* and *Grace Abounding to the Chief of Sinners* have guided many feet into the path of life" (*The Great Controversy*, 252).

Was I ever embarrassed! I went back and read *Pilgrim's Progress* and fell in love with it. Now it is one of my all-time favorites. I may be stubborn, but I'm not stupid.

Sometimes I feel very strongly about what I believe, and that firmness can create problems and misunderstandings. The willingness to try and understand a different or even opposite point of view is not natural to us, and it is only through the grace of God that we will cultivate a willingness to really hear what someone else is saying and to listen without judging them or dismissing their ideas.

All of us come to issues with a different perspective. We have been raised differently, and, yes, we even think differently. One person might be very logical and analytical. If that's not the way we are, the temptation is to discount them, saying, "They are so cold and calculating." Another friend may think with emotions and therefore seem somewhat subjective in his viewpoint. If our thinking is different, we are then tempted to see that person as weak or lacking the moral fiber to make an objective decision. We might even dismiss their ideas because they are not logically driven. We must understand that there are no two human beings who have exactly the same perspective, and often there is nothing inherently wrong in either viewpoint. It *is* wrong, however, to allow division, contention, suspicion, evil surmising, and gossiping to enter into our relationships because of these differences. As wrong as this may be, it is also very human. It occurs in the church and happens between friends all the time. It's sad because we hurt one another needlessly, often over issues that have nothing to do with salvation. We have to learn a better way to deal with these "issues" or we may find ourselves losing our own salvation because of the way in which we deal with one another on these nonmoral issues.

Is it possible for two people, both filled with the Holy Spirit, to see an issue differently? God placed one instance in the book of Acts that we might learn from. Paul and Barnabas had been preaching, and in those days they didn't have it easy. Sometimes I'm tempted to feel I have it hard, that other people are picking on me and don't understand me because they object to my message, but Paul and Barnabas really had it rough. People didn't just object to their sermons; they stoned them, beat them, and had them thrown in jail. Being a minister in those days was not a job for wimps. I sometimes wonder whether the reason there is not that type of persecution today is because we have wimpy men, preaching wimpy messages, about a wimpy salvation, that brings about wimpy results, and only enables their followers to know *about* Jesus, but not really know Him. Thus they will whimper in terror when Jesus returns.

Paul and Barnabas had John Mark with them on one of their preaching trips, but John Mark had a problem. He was like a lot of us. When things got rough, when the way seemed dark and unrewarding, his courage failed him and he ran back home. Paul was not pleased with his behavior, and when the time came to go back and visit the believers in various cities and towns, he refused to take John Mark, the runaway wimp, with him. Barnabas wanted to give John Mark a second chance to prove himself. He and John Mark were related, so he was perhaps more understanding. The Bible records it like this: "And some days after Paul said unto Barnabas, Let us go again and visit our brethren in every city where we have preached the word of the Lord, and see how they do. And Barnabas determined to take with them John, whose surname was Mark. But Paul thought not good to take him with them, who departed from them . . . and the contention was so sharp between them, that they departed asunder one from the other" (Acts 15:36-39).

Even these two godly men struggled with their differing opinions, and God had it recorded so we could see the danger and learn from their mistakes. Is this type of situation happening in your denomination, your church, or perhaps even your own home? Do you have dear ones separating over nonmoral issues? Then you know how it breaks your heart to have it happening to you or to watch it happen to those you love. We may be honest in our understanding of an issue, but when we allow nonmoral issues to cause contention and separation, *everyone* loses.

For years I have known numerous individuals who have loved Sam Campbell's nature books. Sam takes cute and sometimes troublesome forest creatures and often personifies their personalities in a most appealing way. Yet even something that seems so innocent can cause conflict. For example, some parents are uncomfortable with their children reading material that contains personification. I don't want to debate the merits or problems of personification right here. The question is how we relate to one another, if and when we disagree on an issue such as this. And given my experiences with many friends and church members, we do. What if you let your children read these books, and I don't? How will we respond to each other? The problem is that when we differ, the person who doesn't allow their children to read the books is viewed as rather rigid, and the family that chooses to read them is viewed by the nonreaders as rather compromising.

Let's take a couple of families for the purpose of illustration. We'll call the Smiths the rigids, and we'll call the Joneses the compromisers. The Joneses and Smiths were really good friends before the issue of Sam Campbell books came up. In fact, their friendship started because they had so many similarities and common interests, but then they began to see little differences. And as is the tendency in human nature, they began to dwell on the little differences until they came to see them as flaws. Then they added labels such as *compromiser* or *rigid*. Comments were heard such as, "We just can't understand why the Smiths don't see it this way," because, of course, they want others to side with them. Meanwhile, the devil smiles. He loves it. He did it to Paul and Barnabas, and he is doing it to us today.

Do you believe that in a situation such as this, the Smiths and the Joneses can be equally sincere and honest in their view? I do. As time goes on, another issue comes up. This time it is mixed swimming. Just so you understand, we are talking about men and women, boys and girls swimming together in an appropriate setting and with modest attire. Well, the Smiths shy away from such activity because it makes them uncomfortable, and the Joneses don't even realize it's an issue until the Smiths don't come to their swimming party.

Slowly but surely, a degree of intolerance starts to grow, and a wall forms between the two families. As different issues come up that they don't agree on, the wall gets a little higher, until suddenly the children hear their parents talking negatively about the other family. As they see the cold reserve their parents have, they start to imitate it, and the wonderful friendships they had with the other children just aren't the same anymore.

Both families are troubled in their hearts about the situation. They say, "Why can't we get along anymore? We all believe the same things." In their frustration and desire to save the friendship, they decide they need to spend more time together, but what can they do that no one will object to? The zoo! Perfect! So they head to the zoo together on a Monday.

They arrive at the zoo, and for a while it seems like old times. Everyone is enjoying the three-day weekend they created, and because it's a weekday, there are no crowds. Mr. Jones starts to relax and forget about the problems they have had and can't wait to see the gorillas. He has always loved gorillas. There is just something about them that appeals to him and always has. So when they head toward the primate village, he's as excited as the kids.

Recently renovated, the gorilla exhibit is a very popular attraction. As part of the renovation, the designers have created a special observation platform that brings you face-to-face with these marvelous creatures. It is designated for children only, so their view will not be blocked by the taller adults. Now when Mr. Jones sees the sign that reads "Children Only Beyond This Point" he thinks to himself, *That sign is there for a reason, but there are no other children besides ours, so I can't block anyone's view. I'm going to go closer and see the gorillas with the kids.* So he goes down into the children's area and has a great time. The only problem is that the Smiths don't quite see it that way. They believe the sign means what it says. First it's the books, then it's the mixed swimming, and now this compromiser is violating zoo rules. And he is supposed to be a Christian! Clearly this guy isn't fit company for anyone who has respect for the laws of God or man. The cold reserve continues to grow, and they see each other less and less often afterward, and when they do, it's just not the same.

Does this story seem silly to you? This really happens, friends. If you could sit down with the Smiths, I am sure the sentiment in their hearts would be, "I just wish they understood where we're coming from." I don't think they truly want to force their way on the Joneses or anyone else, but they do want to be understood. If you could also sit down with Mr. Jones, he would probably say, "I only wanted to see the gorillas. We didn't know they didn't like mixed swimming. I don't want them to give up their convictions or opinions, but please understand where we are coming from too. We looked at these 'issues,' seriously looked at them, and we don't see any problem with them."

But because we don't like to deal with things openly and honestly, with concern for the other person, our friendships continue to break up. I am going to be bold here and tell you that all of us have some Joneses and Smiths and John Marks in our relationships. Think of some of your friends. Don't you have some who are compromising, too easy going, too liberal? I bet you also have other friends who are too rigid, too disciplined, too black and white, and too stern. Perhaps we even call them behaviorists. And then we see the John Marks as weak, vacillating, prone to discouragement, and unfit for the work. When I go through my mind, I can easily plug in names of families into all those categories. Can't you?

Through the years I have watched what happened with the Smiths and Joneses over and over again until I started calling it "The Three-Year Syndrome." Here is how it works. A couple of families—perhaps yours and and another family in your church, get acquainted, and you find that you have a lot in common. So you socialize with each other and get along great for the first year. But in the second year, you start to find there are some areas you don't see quite the same, whether it is over zoo rules, books, or whatever. You can plug in whatever nonmoral issue you can think of. I bet you know what the issue is in some of your friendships already. The Holy Spirit has a way of bringing those things to our minds. Then in the third year you start to view each other as rigids or as compromisers. Has this happened to you?

Think about your parents or other older folk you know. They get to retirement age and many, if not most, of them don't get together with their old school friends, don't socialize with the people in the old neighborhood or their employment. They have no more friendships. They have worked through this cycle too many times, and in the end they have no more friends. I am not insisting that it takes three years. Some people will last for a longer or shorter time, but it follows the same general pattern.

The problem is, if we can't learn to get along here, we're not going to get along up there, are we? We can't just have a relationship with Jesus Christ; we must have relationships with one another. If we allow this coming together and separating to continue, after a time there will be no one we can get along with, and we will find ourselves all alone, stubbornly declaring, "At last, only I stand for the truth!" How utterly miserable!

The solution lies in four simple steps that are very hard to put into practice. I wish that there were another way to say it, but this is plain hard because it crosses our self-will in a way that few things do in life.

1. **Deference.**

   This means I let others follow their convictions without giving them the cold shoulder, looking down on them, gossiping to others about them, and simply allow them the liberty to be the individual God created them to be.

2. **Self-control.**

   I must control myself, not their "self," no matter how right I think I am. I can't try and correct their supposed imbalances, opinions, or views. Furthermore, I give up my right to view them as rigid, compromising, or unfit for the work simply because they hold a different view. This will require a constant death to self, but the only way to give others their liberty is to put self-will to death every time it rises and wants to control another.

3. **Mutual forbearance.**

   Forbearance doesn't mean to bear down on someone else but rather to exercise patience. We must show to others the same patient longsuffering that God has manifested toward us. For it to become a part of our life requires a miracle of God's grace in our hearts to overcome natural inclinations to impatience.

4. **Sympathy and empathy.**

This means putting ourselves in another's shoes, feeling what they feel, and being pained because they are hurting. It puts us on common ground. Because Christ came and was tempted in all points as we are, He understands our burdens. There are many in our lives who long for such understanding—a child, your spouse, or someone at church. We need one another.

Paul and Barnabas needed each other. You and I need each other! We need each other for balance. Without you and without a lot of other friends in my life, I become unbalanced, and so do you. I need your input, your suggestions, and I need to listen to them honestly to gain the balance that I need in my Christian experience.

In the end, our positions should not be more important than people, and our gospel is only desired when we can truly love those who don't agree with our positions. Love those people in your lives, especially the ones who don't see it your way. Love them before you drive them forever away, not just from you, but perhaps even from God.

CHAPTER 6

UNITY OR UNIFORMITY

"Behold, how good and how pleasant it is for brethren to dwell together in unity!" Psalm 133:1.

When Sally and I moved to the mountains, there were some other couples living in the area that shared the same goals and values we did. "This is great!" we thought. "We can learn from them." After all, Sally and I had been Christians for just four years. I like to say we were baby Christians just learning to toddle about. We were certainly babes in the faith compared to the other couples who had moved to that remote wilderness valley.

Among them was a family headed by a pastor on a sabbatical. He and his family moved to the wilderness so they could get better acquainted with God. Another family had several children, and their dad had been a parochial school principal. All of us were conservative, health-conscious Christians. We all homeschooled our children and believed the same fundamental doctrines. None of us were against the church; we believed in and supported church organization.

We were sure we had found unity. You should have seen our worship group the first few times we got together. Sally and I were on cloud nine. "We're all together and believe the same things. How wonderful!" And it was.

But if you had continued to visit us week after week, you would have noticed that all was not well in our perfect group, with its perfect families, in our perfect setting in the wilderness; for it required no great insight to begin to sense the tension, the discord, the strife that roiled beneath the surface. The whole group sensed it, and it bothered every single one of us. I told Sally, "We've got to do something about this." We went to the other families, and all of us decided to have a weekly prayer and Bible study session in addition to our weekend worship to try and bind our group together.

What do you think we decided to study? That's right, *unity*, the one thing we didn't have. I want you to know that the people we were associated with were no dummies. These were smart people with good minds, far more complex than my simple mind, and we studied together from the fall through the spring. The result of that study was that we had further discord, more contention; and to be perfectly honest with you, things were becoming one *big* mess.

Then someone in our group proposed that if we could agree upon the manner in which we would conduct our homes, our recreation, our reforms, our view of church government and our doctrines, then, and only then, could we have unity. It sounded good and reasonable, so we agreed. We tried, every one of us tried, but we failed miserably. In the end we couldn't even agree on the definition of unity.

Everyone there was sincere; every one of us desired it. With so much good will and earnest desire, how could we fail? We failed because we sought for unity in the outward reforms, we sought after it in policy, and we sought after it in church organization. We found uniformity, but unity slipped through our fingers.

Unity never comes as a result of membership in a church, never as the result of joining a ministry or institution, and never as the result of agreeing to certain truths. Unity comes only as a result of different people from different backgrounds and, yes, even with different biases joining themselves to Jesus Christ. Unity is experienced only to the degree to which we are united to Jesus. And that, my friends, is why we failed.

We couldn't grasp hold of the experience of unity because we sought it in the outward instead of seeking to have our lives hid with Christ in God, being dead to self and what we wanted, and letting Him work His will in us. If we had done that, there would have been no need to decide how we should conduct our families. We could have allowed each person to be drawn toward Christ and therefore automatically drawn toward one another.

The problem in our "perfect" group was that Jim Hohnberger was not dead to self. Neither was my wife, and neither, I believe, was any other person in the group. None of us seemed to understand *how* to be dead to self. We understood doctrine, reforms, and prophecy, but self was another matter. In each of us, probably myself more than the others, was a "self" that was alive and trying to control the others. Have you been there? We finally left our worship group and our Bible study to search alone for that experience that eluded us.

We found that to be joined to Christ requires a living, moment-by-moment connection. No mental assent or theoretical under-standing can provide the intimacy of such a connection, any more than knowing about a person makes them your friend. To come near to Christ is to come near each other. When we are being separated from each other, the root cause is always separation from Christ by one or both parties. Only as both seek to know and do the will of God is there true restoration.

We desire unity. But how few of us have really entered into the experience laid out before us in Psalm 133:1: "Behold, how good and how pleasant it is for brethren to dwell together in unity!"

The Bible describes this lack of unity by saying, "For ye are yet carnal" (1 Corinthians 3:3). Then, just in case we might miss the point, the verse continues, "for whereas there is among you envying, and strife, and divisions, are ye not carnal, and walk as men?" If these things exist among you, then, like it or not, you are carnal. *Carnal* means you are partly ruled by God and partly ruled by self, which in the end means that you are in charge.

I'm telling you from hard personal experience and on the authority of God's Word that if envying, strife, and division are among you and you claim to be born again, you are in trouble! When we lack unity, we will never find it in uniformity, so let's deal with the real issue.

If we claim to be saved, to be converted, and to be born again, we ought to be able to answer some practical questions that have nothing to do with doctrines. I want to know, what are you saved from? What are you converted from? And I really want to know what you have been born out of. If you are still in the flesh, still allowing self to rule in your life, then please let me know just what you were converted from. I've had a lot of sincere people tell me, "I was saved back in the fall of such and such a year," and I always respond by asking, "Saved from what?" I think that is a fair question to ask. Would your wife say you are saved? Would your children say you are saved? Would your friends say you are born again?

Have we been lied to by the books we read, and popular Christian culture, or even by our own hearts? Do we think we are someone we are not? God sees things as they are. We are either united to Jesus Christ or we are not. I had sought after unity by trying to come into uniformity with everyone else, but in truth, when I really took a long hard look at myself, I realized the unity could only come about as a result of union with Christ, never to a church and never to a ministry or a group, and *I didn't have it.* Unity between us will exist only in proportion to the closeness each of us has to Christ. I am going to be bold here and tell you bluntly that when there is discord among two who claim to be Christian, one or both have separated from Christ. I remember once hearing a minister talk about counseling people. He said, "I always try and listen very carefully and with empathy, but I am always asking myself and praying that God will reveal to me what the sin is that lies at the heart of this problem, for it is always a sin. If you are having problems with someone, the single greatest thing you can do to resolve the situation is to get closer to Christ."

Jesus is like a tuning fork. If He has tuned my life and your life, when we come together we will be in tune with each other even though we may have never met, because He who fine-tunes our characters is the same, and the tuning fork, His spotless life, is the standard He desires for both of us. The problem comes when I want to do my own tuning, and then when we get together my pitch is set far too low. Many want unity in the church, and they attempt to achieve it by tuning everyone else's life to their own, just like our group in the mountains did, and sadly found out that it never brings unity.

I once had the opportunity to negotiate a real estate deal for another agent, involving a religious sect that lived in a closed community where all the men wore black and all the women, faded blue. I was fascinated because they seemed so united, or at least they did until I got better acquainted with them. I found out they had all kinds of divisions about their pet issues and rules. This group went beyond the Word of God in their restrictions and regulations, and there were some who felt they went too far, and these would sometimes leave for a group that was less strict. Others felt they didn't go far enough, and these often left for another group that was stricter. Like the Jewish church of Christ's day, they had rules and requirements that exceeded those of God. The Jews got so carried away with their rules that carrying a handkerchief was "work" and, therefore, breaking the Sabbath, but if that same handkerchief was pinned to a garment, it was acceptable. The rules were designed to honor God's commandments, but instead they made them a mockery, only showing shortsightedness and narrowmindedness. Surely we don't do this type of thing anymore, do we?

God managed to show us the whole duty of man in ten little rules. Are we reflecting His character, or are we placing restrictions where God places none? Oh, our motives are good, and we are only trying to unite around common beliefs, but the problem of trying to achieve unity by a set of unifying beliefs is the sheer diversity of areas we can disagree about. For example, conflicts arise in the church over all the following: jewelry and makeup, the origin and accountability for homosexuality, methods of child rearing and discipline, as well as proper dress (whatever that means), tastes in music, entertainment, and diet. Courtship and dating is one subject sure to cause conflict, because everyone has a pet theory as to how it should be done. The sports and competition discussion is another subject sure to hit a raw nerve, no matter what your position.

Then, moving away from lifestyle issues, there are disagreements about beliefs such as the role of faith and works, and the style of worship. Even the attitude of the worshiper during prayer can become a burning issue. Likewise, there are people who have a favorite belief that they ride like a hobbyhorse to the exclusion of every other tenet of Christianity. I don't intend to belittle anyone's belief system, but I share these examples to illustrate a point about our diversity. There are some very nice church people just like you and I, who teach that there is no Holy Spirit. Others similarly question the Godhead or the divinity of Christ. A number believe in observing the feast days from the Jewish economy. What version of the Bible to use has nearly started civil wars in some churches. And we are not dealing with fringe lunatics. This is still well within the mantle of mainline conservative Christian churches. Moving further away from the center, there are deliverance ministries, messenger theories, racist religions, and abusive cults, all of which have a fringe that overlaps the sphere of the church and can cause real mischief.

Enough of that stuff. Let's head back to your local church, where there are probably members who support some type of ministry that is independent of any denominational control, while at the same time there are also likely others in the same congregation who oppose such ministries, feeling they undermine support for the organized church. In like manner you might support the idea of a very active role for women as ministers, while other equally sincere friends object strongly.

The list of issues can go on forever, and we haven't even mentioned the nature of Christ, original sin, the exact composition of human nature, what is acceptable recreation, conspiracy theories, claims of apostasy, parochial schools versus public schools versus homeschool. Then of course, if you do homeschool, you can have conflicts with others over which curriculum is best.

And let's not forget that no new church or school has ever been built, no addition been added, without some division of the congregation over the size, cost, design, color, or even style of the addition. Sometimes these divisions persist long after a project is finished. I once heard of a man who so disliked the wrought-iron railing along the church sidewalk that he came to the church in the middle of the night and not only took it down but dragged the heavy section of rail well off into the woods. The next day others arrived at the church and found the rail missing. Then they noticed something, not readily apparent to the man who had done the midnight deed—the distinct drag marks left behind by the heavy railing. With such a clearly marked trail, it was an easy matter to locate the missing railing, which they hauled back to its place and reinstalled.

But it didn't end there! The gentleman, finding the rail back in its place, returned for another bit of late-night redecorating. This time he was determined to dispose of it properly, without a trace. So he attempted to carry away this huge section of iron fence, but hurt his back before he managed to get it out of the parking lot. He was so badly injured that he was out of work for a while, and, of course, everyone quickly realized who the rail thief was.

This man took it into his own hands to overrule the church's decision, and there are many such ones in the church today. We may not be hauling off rails at midnight, but we let other people know that we don't approve of their church attendance or lack of it. We make sure they know that we don't like the way they fulfill their church offices, their doctrine, their reforms, or the way they use their money. Of course, all these attitudes remind us of another area of conflict, in which some people grant liberty to others to be led by God and some use church, state, or personal authority to control their fellowmen. In our desire to control others we, in our modern way, repeat the sin of Uzzah. Uzzah put forth his hand to steady the ark of God and died for his presumption, yet many of us are troubled by his story because his motives seem so pure and good. He was only trying to help, but his disobedience caused his untimely death.

Uzzah decided to do for God what he felt God was incapable of doing for Himself. He decided that *he* had to protect the ark, even though no one was to touch it. The ark had just spent some months as a trophy in the land of the Philistines, where God had amply demonstrated His ability to look after it. In the same way God has demonstrated the ability for thousands of years to guide His people and His church. Still the temptation seems everlastingly before us to think that He can't manage it without our help.

Are we striving to control our fellowmen? I've seen it over and over. I've been involved with it myself. Man-made restrictions that go beyond the Word of God dishonor God and provide a false picture of the very God we are trying to protect and serve with such rules. Second Corinthians 3:17 says, "Where the Spirit of the Lord is, there is liberty." Now this liberty, under grace, is not to be misconstrued as freedom to sin, which is the misuse of Christian license. If someone is violating clear biblical standards, there is a place for church discipline. However, all too often church discipline is applied to behaviors or beliefs that are not clearly outlined in the biblical record. Once a friend told me, "Jim, you are duty bound to obey and follow all the rules, policies, and restrictions that the church votes regarding nonmoral issues. You can feel free to go against the church if your convictions cross their policies on moral issues," he allowed, "but on the nonmoral issues you must comply." He still wants me to do this, and tries to force it on me. This means that if I were in the Jewish church of Christ's day, he would expect me to pin on my handkerchief or be considered a Sabbath breaker.

When preparing this material, I prayed that the Lord would provide me an example of inappropriate uniformity, and God brought to my mind the Gettysburg Address. "What has that got to do with anything?" I questioned.

"Jim, I want you to load it into your word-processing program and run a grammar check on it."

"But, Lord, that is one of the greatest speeches ever spoken. 'Four score and seven years ago our fathers brought forth, upon this continent, a new nation, conceived in Liberty, and dedicated to the proposition that all men are created equal . . . ' It brings tears to my eyes. How can you improve on that? It's stood the test of time!"

My grammar program didn't think so! There were more than fifteen errors, according to the program, including improper sentence structure and sentences that were too long. It wanted me to delete some words and use different wording. Poor Abraham Lincoln! Is the grammar program correct? Technically, yes. But the program is designed to bring about uniformity of structure, and in so doing it makes everything conform to its idea of what is right and wrong. How drab, and how blah!

I thought this might be a fluke, so I loaded the Declaration of Independence next. You know, the one that begins, "When in the Course of human events" and continues, "We hold these truths to be self-evident, that all men are created equal, that they are endowed by their Creator with certain unalienable Rights, that among these are Life, Liberty and the pursuit of Happiness." It goes on, but I get to feeling patriotic and a lump forms in my chest because these documents are God given and the principles they contain are based on the principles of heaven. My grammar program found more than ten errors in it. It didn't like the sentence structure and took issue with some wording. These documents lose their vital significance and uniqueness when they are forced to conform to outside standards, and we are doing the same thing to those about us. We force them to conform to our "grammar programs" and then wonder why we have problems when they demand their God-given liberty.

I was invited to speak at a church in the southeastern United States, and a week before I was due to speak I received a phone call from the people who had invited me. They were concerned. "Jim, we need to warn you about what is going to happen when you come to the church. There is going to be trouble because of the diversity of people who are coming to the meetings."

"What do you mean?" I asked, puzzled.

"Jim, there are going to be people from three different independent ministries there. You know, ministries that are not real supportive of the church. But that's not all. There are going to be some people coming from a local separatist group, and two other self-supporting institutions are sending representatives to attend."

"Anything else?" I queried.

"Yes, Jim. There are going to be some reform church members there, and some non-Christians, and even some local Amish people are coming. What are you going to do, Jim?"

"Why, I am going to preach the gospel of Jesus Christ that saves us from ourselves and saves us in our marriages and families, because that's something we are missing!"

I must admit I was a little worried about how it might come out, but when I stood in that pulpit I was in a church overflowing with people, all dressed differently. You could actually see the differences between the groups without even knowing their beliefs, and there I was up front to share something with them.

"Will you just look at yourselves?" I began. "Look at you! Every group imaginable is represented in this church, and we have all gathered for one purpose and one purpose only—to find the oneness of Christ that we long for, but haven't been able to find in our individual groups. Praise God!" I could just see the smiles on their faces, as I simply loved them all and shared with them the very thing that had been missing in my "perfect" group in the wilderness.

When you and I, no matter how diverse we are or have been from each other, get together for the purpose of finding that oneness with Christ, we can and will find unity in our churches and friendships, in our schools and in our families. Oneness with Christ is the only way to unity. Will you seek it? Will you value it? And will you grant others the liberty to do the same? If we desire to secure our own happiness and liberty we must begin by protecting even our enemies from the cruel or unjust use of authority. If we fail this we will establish an example that will someday reach even ourselves.

CHAPTER 7

GOD'S TOOLBOX

"Come now, let us reason together, saith the Lord" (Isaiah 1:18).

When Sally and I bought our first brand-new house, I never expected that I might face any house repairs. After all, everything was brand new! Unfortunately, within the week the "brand new" sink backed up. I had never fixed a backed-up sink before, but I learned how, and with every home repair, I usually ended up with a new tool or two that had been required to complete the job.

As the years passed and with it a steady progression of houses and problems, my toolbox became quite extensive, and only rarely do I have to purchase a missing tool. Along with my collection of tools has grown my skill in using them, so now most problems leave me undaunted. In a very real sense, I desire the same for you. Throughout this book we have examined our relationships with others, and it seems only reasonable that I provide you the tools to repair the problems you face. But before we open up the toolbox, there are just a couple of things that might be helpful for you to know.

I have found that one of the hardest things about tricky home repairs is finding time to do them. Your relationships are no different. Sally and I go out every day and spend time together on the swing in our yard. We call it "swing time," and while an everyday meeting might be a little much for all your relationships, a commitment of time is necessary. Nothing so hinders a repair or invites slipshod work like the pressure of insufficient time. You might have to turn over to others some jobs that you have just too little time for.

Likewise, you may have to turn over to others some of the relationships you currently have if you are overcommitted. It is better to have a few close friends than a multitude you have no time to maintain and then have to deal with the hurt feelings that always come when someone gets ignored.

Closely related to this issue of time is the need to let other people express themselves fully and not just jump to conclusions. Let me explain. I had a friend who was involved in a minor auto accident, and when he saw the collision unfolding before him, he tensed for the impact and was really sore for days afterward. He limped to work and was clearly pained by his leg, but he dismissed it because, as he said, his back, arms, and even his chest were stiff and sore. Doctors advised anti-inflammatory medicine, and slowly he made progress, except for that leg. It was still sore after everything else had improved. At last he had it X-rayed and found it was fractured! He had walked around for a week on his broken leg because he discounted what it was saying, positive that it was only strained like everything else.

Relationship repairs are the same way. Unless we listen very carefully to the problem and hear what is really being said, not just in the words but what's beneath the words, we will miss the language of the heart. Another friend of mine thought he heard something one day while turning on a light switch. It was just a little snapping sound, barely audible, but he listened. Even though he was busy, he turned off the switch and removed the switch cover to find wires melting and conditions just right to provide a cozy little fire that might have cost him his home. How many men have lost their homes because they couldn't hear the soft sounds of a neglected wife, the first snapping of the fire soon to consume their marriage. All relationships work on the same principles, and if we fail to listen to others, I mean really hear them, sooner or later the fires of anger and disappointment are kindled.

Now I must confess that I don't know everything, and I can't tell you how much this very idea crosses my will, but it's true. I like to rush right into a problem and find a solution. I think I have good ideas, and the temptation is always there to think that if everyone would just do things my way, which is, of course, the right way, then everything would be fine. Yet I need to take time to consult the owner's manual to make sure I am correct in my understanding, and if I am still not sure, then I have found that the best thing to do is to ask an expert. The advice gained can save hours or even days and often lots of money. This same rule applies in our relationships. God has given us a manual that lays out principles to be followed, but sometimes we are just not sure how to apply these to our present situation; therefore, we must consult the expert. We must commune with God before communing with each other. Just as in consulting a manual for tackling home repair, getting His expert advice saves tremendous time and effort because we know we are doing the right thing. With this background, let's open the toolbox of solutions.

The first tool is a builder's telescopic level. In college I studied surveying, so I may know more than most people do about this tool, but I'm sure all of you have seen these being used. One person looks through the telescope while another holds a measuring rod, often a great distance away. This tool provides perspective. It is never fooled by outward appearance.

I once saw a video of what was locally called Gravity Hill in the Midwest. For years, people in the neighboring area liked to drive visitors unaware of this phenomenon to the base of the hill, where they would stop, place the car in neutral, and then coast up the hill. There was really no mystery because the hill was an optical illusion; it was really a gentle downhill slope, not the incline that everyone saw.

Yet perspective is more than just the way in which we see a problem. Surveyors know about light and earth curvature, and knowledge of these natural laws allows them to make highly accurate determinations. Likewise, an understanding of the laws of God allows us to gain a true estimate of problems by seeing them from God's point of view. The hard part is realizing that no matter how much we may dislike a problem or situation, there is nothing that comes into our lives without our loving heavenly Father allowing it. If we accept this, we gain with the knowledge that God not only has a solution for us, but that He is working through this situation to make us better people.

Perspective is a power tool, and it provides wonderful power for the diagnostic work needed with every problem. Perspective allows me to see that conflict is not an evil thing but an opportunity for growth and understanding, both in the mechanics of functioning homes and in our relationships with others. Perspective or the lack of it affects the attitude we use, and attitude is the next tool for exploration.

Like hammers, attitudes come in many varieties, and it is essential that you and I use the right one for the task at hand. There are framing hammers and framing attitudes. A framing attitude is a heavy weight with a textured head that you don't want to get in the way of. A framing attitude works when others are blamed for problems—framing them, so to speak.

But if the blame game fails for any reason, dodging the blame by playing the martyr is the next ploy. While those who wield this hammer have persecuted others in their attitude, all too often they succeed in shifting public opinion into believing that they are the ones being picked on. But those who live by public opinion usually die by it as well. Trying one's case in the eye of the public tends to be a risky proposition at best because such a jury is notoriously capricious. Hence, those who go this route tend to have exciting but short public lives.

Sledgehammer attitudes are easy to spot and are little more than the framing hammer's big, although less sophisticated, older brother.

They set out to crush anyone opposing their will and way. There is nothing subtle about them, no nuances or feints; they simply wear down the opposition by brute force.

The ball-peen hammer tries to get you to conform to its shape as well. Those with this attitude just go about the process more slowly, yet the objective is the same—mold you into what they think is right.

Force does not dominate all the hammer personalities. There are the weak little tack hammers that just can't do much. If they were content to work within their sphere rather than bemoan their weakness, they could do many little tasks that, while not glamorous, would make the world a nicer place to be. Then there are the broken-handle hammers, all taped up and forever complaining about the way they've been handled. Listen, and you will hear them make excuses about how you just don't understand what it is like to have a broken handle!

As long as any of these attitudes predominate, you will fail in your relations with others. What we need to become through the grace of God is very adaptable general-purpose hammers—just big enough to do real work, yet well-balanced and easy to handle. A hammer that is comfortable in our hands, yet gentle enough for the smallest problem. We need a strong claw to remove those bent nails of division that our brother and sister hammers have driven carelessly, causing the fibers that should hold us together to come apart in ugly splits. A general-purpose hammer doesn't try to force things. It knows the only chance of a solution is to carefully apply its power. This solution-oriented tool is a must for those who would excel regardless of their profession.

My friend Dave is a plumber, and one day I had a chance to watch him work on a pump. He spent a couple of hours on the job, but of those two hours, only ten minutes or so were wasted looking at the problem. All the rest of his time was spent working for a solution. Never once did he blame anyone for the problem, even though it meant he had to work with some incredibly nasty water.

He ignored the mess and only worked toward a solution. You and I need to become just like him. Once a problem is discovered and stated, all our efforts need to be focused upon finding a solution and not on the nasty mess. Becoming solution oriented does not mean a "my way or the highway" solution. No, it is an honest seeking after a resolution that is not only pleasing to both parties but is also pleasing to God.

The next tool is the stethoscope, which allows us to hear under the surface. I once parked next to a friend who is talented mechanically. He loves to tinker with engines, and before I could turn off my engine, he asked me to open the hood of my car while it was still running. I had no idea why, but I complied and watched as he listened carefully and manually increased the engine tempo a time or two, before he informed me I had a problem. Now I want you to understand that I couldn't hear the offending noise, even when he described it to me. However, I trusted his judgment and took the car to the dealership. They listened too and gave exactly the same diagnosis—bad bearing. How did they hear that? I still couldn't. They had a listening heart and were open to the cry of my engine. I was so accustomed to the sound that I had tuned it out. When I used a mechanic's stethoscope, I could hear the noise of the bad bearing too. It was just that I wasn't sensitive and didn't know what to listen for.

In our friendships we have the same problem. We aren't sensitive to the little noises of things going wrong in others. Often we are entirely focused on our need to get from point A to point B. We need the stethoscope of God's Spirit enlightening our minds and showing us what we are missing the same way my friend showed me what I had been missing with my car. Failure to allow God to improve our hearing will doom us to a life of continually doing inadvertent damage to others because we simply don't hear that they are hurting.

When a doctor uses a stethoscope to listen to my heart, he must get close to me—intimate if you will, and must listen beneath the surface to my heart. We must also probe deeply, listening beneath the surface of the words of others, or we will never get to the heart of the matter.

Now we move on to those all-important little things. Our toolbox contains multiple screwdrivers, nut drivers, and wrenches for dealing with the little screws and nuts and bolts of life that always seem to be coming loose. The key to the proper use of these tools is willingness. Anyone can repair any number of annoying loose ends *if* they put their mind to the task prayerfully. When someone brings one of these little problems to your attention, yield it up at once. It is as simple as that. After all, it is only a little thing, easily given up if we have died to self, and not worth holding on to. These things seem so little, yet if they cross the self, it can mean a struggle for us. But what a powerful message they send to others about how we value their worth and their value to us when we surrender to their concern or take their advice.

The measuring tape of God's Word is the next tool. Do I really love my neighbor as myself? In communication with others, it is wise to hold to the old carpenter's edict to measure twice and cut once. Too many times we cut others with our words and actions and only then decide to measure our choices by the measuring tape of God's Word. But then it is too late.

Now we come to the level. Am I keeping my relationships on the level? By this I don't mean just being honest. That should be a given. I mean holding others in a position equal to us. It means not talking down to them or even using body language to convey an attitude of superiority. The failure to demonstrate any value for the other person or what they have to say closes the door to communication. Conversation is like water; it flows best downhill and will only flow uphill if force is applied. If you find your exchanges with others tend to be very forceful, it could well be that they detect in you a superior attitude and it's like trying to make water go uphill. Try leveling the field and see whether a lot of force drops off when you do. There are always exceptions, but few people will fight if you don't provide them something to fight against.

At last we come to an item too big to fit inside our toolbox, and that is the workbench. There are times when you have tried every option you can think of without resolution. When this happens, perhaps because it's a particularly difficult situation or a really stubborn problem, then you have little choice but to place the problem on the workbench to be resolved at some point in the future. Time can be a magic cure for many conflicts. If we return to a problem that we have mutually agreed to set aside for an hour, a day, a week, or more, we often come back with a new perspective and maybe even new ideas. By putting an item on the workbench, "tabling it," tempers have a chance to calm down.

This isn't an easy thing for me to do because I'm a stubborn German. At times I have found myself so frustrated in some repairs that I wanted to kick the bench, and you may have felt the same. I won't ask whether you have actually kicked some very inflexible inanimate objects. At those times my only safety is to leave it alone and retreat to God.

If we will leave an unsolved problem on the workbench and love the person with whom we have a conflict, we gain hope that even if we can never find a solution or permanent repair, our relationship and mutual respect will be stronger than our problem.

I once met a man who loved to tinker with anything and everything. How do I know? His basement was filled with the carcasses of every item he had ever worked on, tried to repair, or had stored away in the hope that its parts might be useful. I even saw him pulling a part off a neighbor's junk car just before the junkyard came to pick it up. No, he didn't have a car like it, but he was afraid there might come a day he'd need that very part.

Don't be too hard on him, because while he will never use the stuff, most of us are just like him. We want to hold on to the past as if yesterday's garbage will be today's treasure. Leave the past in the past. I don't know about you, but when I have an electrical problem in my home I don't want it fixed with thirty-year-old second-hand parts. The same is true of relationships. Leave the past alone. If there is a problem currently, deal with it currently, and don't fall into the trap of bringing up the past. Just like those old parts in my friend's basement, no good can come from bringing them up.

Super glue is the last-ditch item that we resort to when all else has failed. If we cannot come up with any solution and we find ourselves still far apart in spite of honest efforts on both sides, then it is sometimes possible to break through by accepting the blame. Bear with me for a moment. I haven't lost my senses.

I'm sure each of us would like to view ourselves as perfect. However, chances are that at least in some small way, we are at fault for the situation in which we find ourselves. Only God knows to what degree we caused the mess, but we can choose to accept all the blame if we want. Christ did this for us, and if it might help redeem another, how can we do less? This doesn't mean we give up our positions, principles, or ideas, but it does mean we take upon ourselves the burden of having caused the misunderstanding. Accepting all the "blame" and seeking forgiveness of the other party is an extraordinarily healing act. It is like super glue; it binds the parties together! However, it works only if done with sincerity and heartfelt meaning. If you act the part of the martyr, you might as well have never spoken because people—even when they disagree with you—can tell when you are speaking from the heart and when an action is not sincere.

What if you have a relationship in which every tool fails and you still can't see eye-to-eye? Then let the other person have the freedom to pursue God, as they understand Him, and grant each other the liberty to be led separately of each other. Two cannot walk together unless they are agreed. So walk separately if need be, always holding yourself ready for God's timing to resolve your dispute at a later date. Paul the apostle and John Mark did get back together in the end, and I know this is God's desire for every one of us. Use this toolbox of solutions, and *some* of your relationship problems will disappear. Use these tools under the guidance of the Spirit of God, and *most* of your relationship problems will disappear. It is my prayer that God may use these simple tools to work a mighty project in your life and build many beautiful relationships. For in the end, relationships are not about ideas, positions, or conflict—they're about people!

CHAPTER 8

LOVE WITHOUT AN "IF"

"By this shall all men know that ye are my disciples,
if ye have love one to another" (John 13:35).

When I was first introduced to God's Word I fell in love with it. I wasn't in love with Jesus because I didn't know Him, but I saw in His Word a beauty, an order, and an unfailing guide for my life. I set out to do all that I read in His Word. I did everything in my power—I didn't know there was anything else. I didn't know how to surrender or to give my choices to Jesus.

I took the little I knew and said, "Lord, I am going to do what You want me to." I had found the truth, and I understood the Bible, or at least I thought I did. Even the little bit I did know seemed so much better than what I had known before. I sincerely thought this was all there was to being a Christian. I thought I had arrived and was happy.

But God wasn't happy. He is never happy until we receive the very best from Him. He let me know that there were some things in my life that weren't reformed, and when this was clear I set out determined to make these changes. Now I'm stubborn and I'm a full-blooded German. I've got a strong will and I am not afraid to use it, but what I didn't understand back then was that my strong will is to be used to surrender to Jesus, not to accomplish what Jesus was asking me to do. I was sincere, and I really tried, but at home it always broke down. I always lost it in my home, with my wife and family. I couldn't fake it there as I could elsewhere. In our home we did all the things that conservative Christians are supposed to do. We had worship, listened to good music, dressed right, and even homeschooled, yet somehow the essence of true Christianity—that is, a real change in the heart, gaining the victory over self, and the transformation of the home attitude and spirit—was lacking. We had the reforms, all the outward trappings of Christianity; we even had success in evangelism, but after four years in the church, God told me, *"Jim, I want you to move out to the mountains, and there I want to really show you the gospel. I want to do this because you have been doing a lot in your own strength, and you look good on the outside, and the people in the church think you're great, but your wife doesn't, and your children don't, and I don't either!"*

I had been doing my own religion, and when I got out to the wilderness I was confused. I had heard all these theological terms, and I didn't really know what they meant—not experientially, not as they related in a personal way to my life—and God told me to put them all away. When you read one of my books, or hear one of my messages, you will not get a lot of theological terms, and that is why. God showed me that all He wanted from me was my choices. He wanted me to surrender my will to Him and then allow myself to remain submitted to Him, abiding in Him, resting in Him, enjoying Him, loving Him as children love their parents and allow the parents to carry all the burdens of life for them. Suddenly, as I started to implement this new concept of religion, God became a very real and caring part of my daily existence.

Looking back on my past attempts at witnessing, which amounted to simply converting people to the truths of the Bible but never introducing them to God on a personal level, I stand amazed at just how simple and clear the gospel really is. With this knowledge came the shocking understanding that I wasn't the only one missing the true gospel. Almost every church and minister are missing the simplicity and practicality of the gospel.

"This is it, Lord! This message You have shown me here in the wilderness—this is the real gospel that I have longed for!" It was so simple, and yet the effects were so profound that it went beyond doctrine, way past witnessing to others, and it fully eclipsed my old "do-it-yourself" religion. I was excited, and God rejoiced with me, but God wasn't finished with Jim Hohnberger.

More recently God is showing me that having Him as a moment-by-moment part of my life, as important and vital as that is, just simply is not enough. He has made it clear that even being at peace with Him by repentance from every sin He has made known to me and having made right every wrong that I humanly can with my fellowman, is not sufficient. He has told me that the preaching of this wonderful message does not imply that Jim Hohnberger is fully or even partially reflecting the image of his Maker. None of these is enough for God. God has shared with me that I am still unbalanced in my thoughts, ideas, and, most of all, my experience. I need to learn to love others without an "if."

You see, it is not enough for me to love Jesus completely and fully without reservation. This kind of love is rare enough, and it is pleasing to God, but it is hardly complete. If we were to look at it as reflected in the Ten Commandments, this love for God is epitomized in the first four commandments, but what about the other six? God has shared with me that I must learn to love others, not just those who are my friends, the ones who are easy to love, but also those who disagree with me, those who are my enemies!

"You must learn to love others unconditionally, whether they disagree with you or not. I want to bring you into this experience, Jim. Will you let Me?"

I said, "Lord, how far does this gospel of Yours have to go?"

I want to share with you what God showed me when I asked this question. He took me to Romans 5:6, 7. "For when we were yet without strength, in due time Christ died for the ungodly. For scarcely for a righteous man will one die: yet peradventure for a good man some would even dare to die." Who are these ungodly people? That's you and me! When I was without strength, unable to love Him, unwilling to even respond to Him, Jesus died for my sins and yours. For every person who has lived or will live, Jesus willingly took their sins, even in the full knowledge that most would never love Him in return. The verse then talks about some being willing to die for a good man, and that is true. You and I are willing to risk much for people we perceive as being "good." They may be fellow human beings unknown to us personally, but we instinctively assess them as good people like ourselves, and we would try to save them from danger, just as we would want them to do for us should the roles be reversed.

Recently, the world watched and honored the firefighters and other emergency-service personnel whose last recorded images are snapshots in smoky stairwells of the World Trade Center as they trudged up while everyone else tried to escape, and almost 400 of them died as heroes trying to save others. This self-sacrifice demonstrates the very best ideals in the United States, but would we see it as virtuous if they had lost their lives when the only people to be saved were the despicable criminals who had caused this catastrophe? I don't think we would risk the loss of even one firefighter to save those evil men. That is just human nature.

"But God commendeth his love towards us, in that, while we were yet sinners, Christ died for us" (verse 8). Loving those who can't do anything for you or who will not do anything for you is beyond the pale of human experience and entering into the Divine. Oscar Schindler, a German manufacturer, who worked ceaselessly to protect his Jewish workers during the long years of the Nazi death camps, once rescued hundreds of his female employees from certain death in Auschwitz. Years later, realizing what Schindler had done for them, one of the rescued said, "He was our father. He was our mother. He was our only faith. He never let us down." She had come to know the love that Schindler had toward his workers, and this had awakened in her the most profound gratitude. God works the same way to win our hearts and minds. He says, "Jim Hohnberger, I am going to do everything for you. I am going to pour out My soul unto death for you, in hopes of winning your heart."

"While we were yet sinners Christ died for us." Who is the "us" mentioned here? Did Christ die for the conservatives? He did, you say. Well, what about the liberals? Them too? What about the moderates, church leaders, ministry leaders, pastors, and separatist leaders? What about other denominations, including those we may not agree with, or the ones we view as little more than cults? Did Jesus die for them too? What about the Jews, the Muslim extremists, the pope? Christ gave His life for us whether or not we joined His church or His religion. He gave His life for us without conditions. Jesus treated Judas the same as He treated Peter. What would you do with Judas, knowing as Christ did that the final outcome of all your efforts for him would still lead to betrayal? Jesus shows no partiality, but what about us?

Jesus loved others without an "if." He didn't say, "If you change, I'll love you." Jesus' love was poured out for me before I ever made a single change. Jesus didn't say, "If you accept My theology and doctrines, then I'll love you." Jesus didn't say, "If you accept My reforms and lifestyle and enter into them, then I will love you." He didn't say that to me, and He has never said that to anyone. But what do we say to others?

Jesus didn't say in attitude or word, "If you see things the way I do, Jim, then I will love and accept you." Jesus didn't say, "If you do things My way then I will minister to you and your needs." Jesus didn't say, "If you follow in My steps, then I will help you, perform miracles for you." He didn't have the petty attitudes that so mark our behavior toward those we claim to minister to. Jesus went right up to Roman officers who had the backing of the full might and power of the entire empire. He healed them as willingly as He did anyone else, because He loved them as people. He didn't decide that He wasn't going to minister to someone because of the position they held. Jesus' love passed over the politics of His day, the politics of His church, and the politics of His people. He dared to love and minister to everyone with no exceptions, whether they were in the church or outside the church, liberal or conservative, saint or sinner, unchurched or at odds with the church. Shame on us for our shallow, puny, surface love with a great big "if"!

We say it this way: "I'll love and minister to you if you join my church." What is our motivation in evangelism? Are we really there to love other people? If the truth were told, most of what passes for outreach is a display of conditional love—love with a big "if." Think back on the last few outreach campaigns your church has run and look at the amount of true ministry done for those who may have attended some or all of the meetings, but rejected the offer to join the church. I don't mean adding their names to a mailing list or inviting them to special services, but truly ministering to their needs. I think you will have the answer about the type of outreach being done. If our efforts are only for those who will join with us, then we love with an "if" and have much to apologize for to those we have wronged in our so-called outreach. We have displayed not the attributes of God but of self-interest.

I know a lot of conservatives who, if I will agree with their views, will accept and love me, but if I won't agree with them, they won't give me the time of day. No wonder we are not winning the world! Unlike Jesus, we say, "I will love and minister to you if you will accept my lifestyle and my reforms." There is many a person who would just fall in love with my family if we would accept their fanaticism, but if we don't, boy, do they look down their noses at us. Is that the gospel? Is that what Jesus has called us to?

In saying we will love you if you'll follow our rules, regulations, and guidelines, we claim one thing but we do another. We say we follow the Bible and the Bible only. We claim *sola scriptura* as our motto, but we have another dozen or so man-made rules and policies that you must abide by as well. If you don't, then you are not going to get along very well in our church. If you don't you won't be looked upon very well in our church and will find yourself at odds in our organization. Is that reflecting Jesus Christ?

I am not talking about lowering standards. Heaven forbid such a thing. Jesus Christ had the highest standards of anyone who ever lived in this world, but He did not throw others out because they did not have the same standards. What a love God has for us. We must ask ourselves the question, Is much of what we do simply designed to meet our needs while supposedly ministering to others' needs?

Our motivation in evangelism should be to connect them with Jesus, who can ransom their souls, but usually our motive is the desire to get others to believe as we do. We want them to think like us, to join with us, to be just like us, to support us and our ideas. It is not *love,* my Christian brothers and sisters. It is not love to try and make people over in our image instead of the image of God.

Love, as God displays it, is the giving of ourselves entirely for the benefit of others. That is Heaven's definition of love, and if it is applied, it resolves problems like nothing else. I have counseled with countless couples and families over the years, and in *every* case, the problem in the home is that the husband will not live entirely for the benefit of the wife, and the wife will not live entirely for the benefit of the husband, and neither of them will put themselves out for the children. And with no example the children never learn to live for their parents or each other. The way you live for others demonstrates the love you have in your heart. We have the love of

God when we can live entirely for that church that is following the ways of the world; when we can live entirely for that ministry that we don't agree with. Then and *only* then do we have a power that can pull that church back from the world or that ministry into a more balanced position. Loving this way is a commitment to love when there is nothing in it for me, nothing in it for the church, nothing in it for my ministry, and nothing in it for God. God loves when there is nothing in it for Him! It is just His nature to love—without an "if."

If Jesus were among us today, He would love everyone the same and minister to and associate with every group. He would minister to the organized body of believers, to those who have church at home, to those who are only on the fringe, to every misguided soul with their photocopier putting out a newsletter, and He would do it because He is the God of love. He would love those ministries that are independent and not part of a denominational system. He would even love and minister to the unchurched and the betrayers like Judas. Are there any betrayers in your life or your church? Have you found the type of love that can truly care for that type of person? He would love and minister to the backsliders and those who are hard to love. Are there any in your life who are hard to love?

Revelation 14:6 says, "I saw another angel fly in the midst of heaven, having the everlasting gospel to preach unto them that dwell on the earth, and to every nation, and kindred, and tongue, and people." If we are to be part of the movement here described, it's not enough to know about the gospel, of the gospel, or even have a degree from a great university stating we have a doctorate in gospel studies. No, we must *have* the gospel; it must be a part of us. The gospel message described in this verse is taken to every part of the world, every nation, kindred, tongue, and people. I see no exclusions. No one is left out or considered unworthy.

What is "kindred"? I looked it up, and I loved what I found. It is an offshoot. The gospel is for the offshoots! And yet, I had a church leader tell me we shouldn't minister to the offshoots. We are missing the gospel of Christ when we speak this way. Anyone who doesn't want the gospel to go to those who need it the most has never tasted of the love of God themselves, and they need to be loved. So don't throw them out! Love them instead!

"To every nation" means there are no language barriers, no biases regarding color or social standing. "To every people" does not imply just those who make us feel comfortable. I know a lot of people outside the organized church who will be glad to love and minister to those who think like they do, but they look down at anyone associated with the corrupt organized body. And I know a lot of church leaders who refuse to have anything to do with those people outside the church whose views are a little different from theirs, and they look rather disdainfully on those trouble-some people. Both groups have the same problem. They are missing the gospel, and until they find it, they are going to continue to stand for their separate truths while missing *the* truth, the *only* truth that can set them free. When we pick and choose whom we will minister to, our actions say, "I will have nothing to do with them." But how are the "them" ever going to get the gospel if we won't associate with them? If this is our attitude, perhaps the real question we must ask ourselves is how are *we* ever going to get the gospel if we won't associate with them? Jesus' ministry bypassed the prejudices of His church, the biases of His nation, and the bigotry of the politics of His day. His love reached out to every-one. His love reached out even to me, and it reaches out still to this very day.

Jesus knew that in the end His church was going to be made up of people from very different backgrounds and experiences, but they would have two things in common. I am not thinking of the criteria in the book of Revelation that you might quote to me, because the criterion I am speaking of is the prerequisite for the possession of what John, who wrote Revelation, was speaking of. Jesus also shared two criteria that the true in heart would meet, and you can read about it in Luke 10:27: "Thou shalt love the Lord thy God with all thy heart, and with all thy soul, and with all thy strength, and with all thy mind." Everything—that's what God wants from Jim Hohnberger, nothing withheld, nothing between us. He draws me so close that He covers my imperfect character with His robe of righteousness. And as He holds me so close, He speaks to me there and explains: *"Your past means nothing, Jim. I've already paid the price for you. I have given you the power to choose to be so close to Me that My robe may cover you and all the scars that sin has left. When My Father looks upon you now, all He sees is My spotless character. Now will you stay with Me, Jim? I've given you the power to choose to stay with Me. Apart from your choice to stay with Me, you are helpless to do what you would. But if you choose to surrender your will to Mine, and I have made it possible for everyone to do that if they want to, then My Grace can control your actions through the faith you are exercising. You can do it, Jim. Like everyone who has ever lived from Adam on down, I have given you the power to decide to stay with Me. It is your choice, your birthright as a child of God, to come to Me and be covered by My character and My righteousness and then stay with Me and let Me keep covering you. I won't make you, but I want you to. Will you do it, Jim?"*

"Thou shalt love the Lord thy God with all thy heart." That is the easy one, friend. I've come to the point where I have given God everything I know how to yield. That doesn't mean there isn't room for this experience to grow and deepen, but it does mean that for the stage in life that I am in, I am fully surrendered to God. But God has shown me there is another layer of self to be dealt with. *"Jim, I want you to love thy neighbor as thyself."*

That's a hard one to do. That's why in the Ten Commandments loving God takes only four commandments while loving our neighbor consumes the other six. God is very lovable, and it is easy to love Him. I can go up in the mountains and spend four days with God and I don't want our special time together to end. But with some folk? I don't know whether I would want to spend four hours up in the wilderness alone with them, let alone four days! They're just not that lovable as friends. How do I love unlovable people as I love myself? It is all about my choices. Jesus promises me that if I yield up my choices to Him, He will give me the power to love everyone, even stubborn old Germans like Jim Hohnberger.

Once a leader in the church of His day, upon hearing this truth from Jesus, asked Him a speculative question. There are a lot of such questions running about the church, and the man wanted to use this one to try and distract Jesus from bringing the truth too close to home. He inquired, "Who is my neighbor?" In other words, just how far does this love have to go?

In response Jesus told the beautiful parable of the good Samaritan. A man who was traveling fell among thieves who had beaten him nearly to death, robbed him of all that he had, even the clothes on his back, and left his bloodied form to die in the roadside ditch. Then came a man, a leader in God's church, along the same pathway, and seeing the man, he crossed over to the other side of the road and looked away. He walked on, his step lively and his hand upon his purse lest he too become a victim. Did he have the gospel?

Then another man, well respected in the town and church, passed by, and he saw the man, his chest still feebly rising, but noticed that he was clearly of the working class, not a professional. He looked at his own fine clothes and at the stranger covered in wounds. The prospect of touching him was so distasteful that he involuntarily shuddered. The man was almost dead and would surely die anyway.

Already flies and gnats were gathering round the wounds, and soon vultures would perch in nearby limbs. If he touched him and the man later died, he might well be considered ceremonially unclean. No, better to leave him where he was, poor chap, to die in peace, the man decided.

The Samaritan trader was tired as he led his animal up the mountain pathway. He had to cover a lot of ground if he were to make any money, given the tax rates of the Romans and their crooked tax collectors. A movement suddenly distracted him from his thoughts. Something in the roadside ditch had moved. It looked like a dead creature of some sort, maybe not quite dead, but it wasn't quite right either—too pale, too white for any wild animal. Then it dawned on him.

Rushing to the scene, he was confronted with a pitiful sight. The man in the ditch was a Jew, a rival sect to the Samaritans. They believed in the same God and their worship was similar, but they didn't agree on some of the finer points of doctrine and practice, and the contention between the groups had been long and bitter. Still, he couldn't let this man die here in the road, so tearing his spare garment he bound up his wounds and managed to get some water down the parched throat. Then with great difficulty he loaded him on his beast and struggled into the next town as the sun set. A howl of a wolf echoed in the darkening hills behind them, as if he mourned the loss of an easy meal.

The Samaritan man faced choices. He had to work hard and get dirty, pay for the medicine and the man's care. And the man was probably completely opposed to his positions. Jesus asked the questioner in His day, which was neighbor unto him who fell among the thieves? Today He might ask, who will be a neighbor to the one who leaves the church, the one who disagrees with you, the one who has become fanatical, or even the sinner who dared to have an open affair?

What a rebuke to the prejudice and biases you and I have toward those we don't agree with. Our neighbors are *not* just those we like or those who view things our way. Jesus' church and Jesus' love are not as narrow as our conception. Christ's church is going to be made up of a Nicodemus, who found Jesus secretly at night, and some like Joseph of Aramathaea, who was a secret disciple of Jesus for fear of the Jews. There will be a lot of church leaders who, while they seem part of an outwardly corrupt church, are secret disciples of Jesus, and we must remember that God looks not on the outward appearance as we do but on the heart. Many of these men will come through, just as Joseph did, when things look the bleakest for the church. Jesus' church will have some rough, unlearned fisherman types like Peter. He was a fearless follower of his Master, and he felt it too great an honor to die like Jesus so he asked to be crucified upside down. Christ's church will include tax collectors—government employees. So many on the edges of Christianity look with suspicion upon any government agent or law enforcement officer as an operative for some one-world government. They ask me, "What are you going to do, Jim, when they swoop down on you in their black helicopters?"

I'm not going to run from them, I'll tell you that! My Lord faced all the fury and hate that the kingdom of Satan could bring against Him and stood fast in the midst of the storm and won many hearts to Himself that day. By His grace I would not want to see one Christian run away from such a conflict as though guilty of something other than being good and pure men and women through the indwelling of God's Spirit in the human heart. If someone wants to arrest me or kill me because I am a Christian, then they can do it, but only if my Lord allows; for my life is in His hands, and nothing can befall me unless He allows it. However, if someone wants to arrest me, they are going to hear about the gospel.

Christ's church is going to be made up of some who were blind, some who were lepers, some who were demon possessed, some who had problems with anger management, as we'd say these days, but back in His day they just called them the "sons of thunder"! What kind of power is it in this message that draws so many diverse people toward the same goal?

In the end all these people will have one common denominator, that they all love other people as much as they love themselves. Jesus said if you love one another then shall all men know you are My disciples, and if that is the criterion, and His words are true, then you and I have a very long way to go if we are ever to be fit for the kingdom. This type of love cannot be manufactured by us, cannot be faked, and is utterly worthless when pretended in public. Only by abiding in Christ, by beholding His love, and allowing Him to alter our characters, can our puny love be changed into a love after His image. Don't point to your church affiliation, because church affiliation is not enough. Don't rest in your beliefs or your theology, because assent to truth is not enough. Don't even try to rest comfortably in your reforms and lifestyle changes, thinking you have obtained what God has for you, because they aren't enough either. Certainly don't rest securely in your attendance and support of *any* church, because it is not enough.

Remember, it was not the churched, not those widely perceived as good people, who made it through in Christ's day. And I declare before the whole world that if all you have are the forms of Christianity, if all you have is the reputation of a saint, if all you have is strong human effort to do right, then you, on the basis of history and divine revelation, are in mortal danger, for only those who are like their Master in words, actions, and motivations will at last be saved because they have learned to love without an "if."

Don't think I am throwing out good lifestyles, nor am I removing the place of doctrine and belief. I am just putting them in their proper sphere. We need His love. After telling the story of the good Samaritan,

Jesus tells us to go and do likewise. In other words, go and live entirely for the benefit of others.

I cannot think of a better illustration of this type of love than the story I once heard of Deena and Paul. It is a true story that took place in the 1960s, and yet it speaks powerfully to us today.

Paul was a man's man. He was tall and handsome, the former football star turned high-school coach. Not only was he a superb physical specimen, he had an intellect to go with it, and even more important, character. He had high ideals and old-fashioned morals. When he was twenty-five years old, Paul fell in love with the home-coming queen. She was equally smart and shared the same high morals. She was popular and had a vivacious spirit that attracted Paul and won his heart. Both were religious, and the conduct of their courtship gained the approval of the whole community. They were going to have a storybook wedding and live happily ever after as the perfect couple and raise wonderful children. Everybody knew it, and everybody expected it, but something happened outside the realm of the happy world they expected, something over which they had no control—Vietnam.

And, of course, Paul volunteered for service. He didn't have to go, but he loved his country and enlisted anyway. He felt a duty to serve the country he loved, and he entered officer's basic training. When he graduated as a brand-new lieutenant, he married Deena. Then he was shipped out for an assignment in the jungles of Vietnam as a reconnaissance patrol leader. He took his men behind enemy lines and would live for days outside the protection of friendly units. Before he finished half of his tour of duty, his group was ambushed, and Paul was so severely injured that it is a wonder he didn't die. He lost his left arm at the elbow. His right hand was a stub except for two fingers that dangled uselessly, and unless the other damage to his arm healed quickly, he probably would lose that limb as well. Perhaps it was better that he couldn't see very well at first, with his gruesome facial injuries and the loss of the left eye. Shrapnel had done so much damage that his features weren't recognizable, his teeth shattered, his nose broken, and what little remained uninjured was hideously swollen. His upper legs and buttocks had been peppered with fragments of metal, but many had to be left in place for fear he wouldn't survive the surgery to remove them. His legs were swollen too, with damaged circulation and jungle rot. There was little chance they would ever carry him again.

Yet the army shipped him back to the States to the medical facility nearest his home. On the way he ran into another army buddy, who tried to cheer him up, saying, "Don't worry, Paul, old boy, the army will fix you up again. The army," he assured him, "has got the best medics and doctors in the world." It was hard to understand Paul's reply through those scabby lips, but he said resignedly, "They've already done their best." And so Paul came home to face whatever would be his future.

Deena was eager to see her love. The staff tried to prepare her, but they knew what was going to happen; they had seen it happen too many times before. The wives would take one look at what was left of the men they loved and without a word would turn around, go home, and after some weeks or months, the paperwork would find its way to the hospital, letting their man know they had filed for divorce.

Deena was different. She never dreamed of leaving him. There was nothing in this for her, no point in loving such a man as this, was there? For Deena, this was still the man she had fallen in love with, and while physically he was not the same, inside was an unscarred Paul, and she loved him. The more he needed her, the more she could prove her love to him. True love goes beyond scars, disappointments, and sorrow. Real love lives only for the benefit of the other.

What would you have done? What are you doing in your family, your church, your home, with those who are not easy to love or who will give you nothing back for your efforts?

Deena was determined to help Paul. She spent every moment she could with him. She took over nursing his wounds and bathing him. She loved him, and made sure he knew she was with him. She was so determined to stay after hours that the nurses at last just looked the other way as she spent long nights caring for him. She loved him through his thirty-one surgeries.

God is doing surgery on you and me as well. Are you going to love me through my surgeries as God prunes my character, or will you abandon me if I am not all you think I should be? God is trying to take us deeper.

Deena gave her time to rehabilitating her husband. Are we willing to give our time to rehabilitate our families, our friendships, our churches, or do we just walk away? Christianity is not a permissive love with an anything-goes attitude; it's a commitment to love by principle even those who don't seem worth loving. It is not just knowing the Life-Giver but walking in His footsteps. It is a commitment to love in spite of the faults, differences, and imbalances that come between us. It is a commitment to allow the Holy Spirit room to work in one another's hearts and in one another's lives without trying to play junior holy spirit.

If we were to put ourselves in the story I just shared, I am the Vietnam vet, and so are you. Jesus Christ is Deena. Jesus sneaks in whenever He can, whenever we will let Him, and ministers to our wounds. He looks at me, the basket case, and says, you are helpless and hopeless, Jim Hohnberger, but your helpless condition only allows Me to prove My love for you.

This is the saving gospel of Jesus Christ. It goes beyond who is right and who is wrong, beyond doctrine and denominational affiliation, beyond reforms and lifestyle changes; it goes beyond last-day events and prophetic understandings. It deals with the very heart of the matter—love without an "if." God is calling you right now with His great love. He is asking you to exercise the same love toward others as He does, not in and of yourselves, for it is not in you, but in a life of choices yielded to Him and allowing Him to put this love in you. This is the power that will change the world, for the gospel is about loving others without an "if." It's about *people!*

"A new commandment I give unto you, That ye love one another; as I have loved you, that ye also love one another. By this shall all men know that ye are my disciples, if ye have love one to another" (John 13:34, 35).

Dear Reader,

Tens of thousands have been thrilled by the story of our family's move to the wilderness, as told in the book *Escape to God*. Truly, the incidents we share in this book are a wonderful, life-changing story. However, they represent only a handful of the incredible adventures we went through in coming to the quiet. My next book will help you explore with us the rest of the story—events that sent our hearts soaring; incidents so funny they still make us rock with laughter; and the wonderful people and creatures that became our friends and neighbors.

Yet there was another side too. The wilderness served us bone-numbing cold and backbreaking work. It provided deeply personal conflicts that left our spirits crushed, and in the end it provided a nursery in which our relationship with God continued to grow.

This forthcoming book is not just a wilderness primer, not just a "how-to" manual, and not propaganda to move everyone to the wilderness. This is a book about an experience that can be gained anywhere. It is about a state of mind as much as a state of being. In the end it is a deeply personal invitation from the Holy Spirit to "Come to the Quiet."

Jim Hohnberger

Other best-selling books from Jim Hohnberger